Special Educational Needs

Special Educational Needs

Marie Delaney

OXFORD
UNIVERSITY PRESS

OXFORD
UNIVERSITY PRESS

Great Clarendon Street, Oxford, OX2 6DP, United Kingdom

Oxford University Press is a department of the University of Oxford.
It furthers the University's objective of excellence in research, scholarship,
and education by publishing worldwide. Oxford is a registered trade
mark of Oxford University Press in the UK and in certain other countries

ISBN: 978 0 19 420037 0

Printed in China

This book is printed on paper from certified and well-managed sources

The publisher would like to thank Special Educational Needs specialist Susan
Hillyard for her contribution at the concept development stage of this book.

Illustrations by: Oxford Designers and Illustrators.

Acknowledgements

Ideas do not exist in isolation. The ideas and activities in this book came out of collaboration and discussion with many great people over the years. I would like to thank all my colleagues and students who have contributed to the learning in this book, in particular Sally Farley for her insight, her unfailing enthusiasm for inclusion, and her excellent chapter on assistive technology.

Thanks to all my colleagues at Pilgrims who over the last 25 years have supported and encouraged creativity and engagement in learning for all, in particular Simon Marshall, Noreen Caplen-Spence, Paul Davis, Judy Baker, Mario Rinvolucri, and the late Bonnie Tsai. My thanks go also to my British Council colleagues Debbie Candy and especially Phil Dexter for his continued support and promotion of this work.

Thanks to colleagues from the Aveley school, where we continually searched for new ways to make learning accessible to those who found it difficult, in particular to Julie Blevins, the LDC staff, and Bernie Thomas for his instinctive knowledge of how to work with parents.

And of course special thanks to all the students and their families who have taught me so much about Special Educational Needs and inclusion.

Thanks to Naomi Moir, Andrew Dilger, Julia Bell, Helen Gyde, and Sarah Finch at Oxford University Press for seeing this book through to the final version.

Last but not least, thanks to my family and my husband, Olly, who remains patient as deadlines approach and stress levels rise. This book could not have been written without him.

Contents

Introduction

Who is this book for?

> I have more and more children with special educational needs in my class and I feel worried about it. I really want to help them, but I'm not sure if I'm doing the right thing. I haven't got proper training in this area, and neither have my colleagues. We all feel a bit lost and confused.
>
> VERA, PRIMARY TEACHER, PORTUGAL

Are you a primary or secondary teacher of English? Do you feel like Vera? At the moment, in many countries across the world, governments are introducing polices of social and educational inclusion. Teachers are being asked to support these policies by teaching students with all types of **special educational needs (SEN)** in their mainstream classrooms. There are many teachers like Vera, who are trying to include these students in their lessons but are worried because they haven't had any specialist training.

A word of reassurance

There isn't a magic formula for teaching students with SEN. Most strategies which help students with SEN are simply good teaching strategies, and you probably know many of them already. You don't need to develop a whole new way of teaching, but you might need to apply your strategies more consistently and consciously to help these students. This book explains the needs of students with SEN and suggests practical classroom strategies to help you to build your confidence in teaching them.

Organization

The book is organized into three parts:
1 Part 1 is an overview of SEN, providing general teaching principles for teaching students with SEN in the mainstream English classroom.
2 Part 2 addresses the general needs of students with SEN, discussing techniques which promote inclusion and dealing with common areas of difficulty.
3 Part 3 provides specific information on individual types of SEN.

The first two parts will give you a general understanding of SEN and successful teaching approaches, while Part 3 can be dipped into according to the type of SEN that interests you.

Scope

The book covers a range of SEN likely to appear in mainstream English language classrooms and does not cover more severe disabilities. The suggested classroom activities can be used for primary and secondary students. There may be techniques which you believe are only suited to younger learners, such as the use of pictures and visuals. This is not the case. All the activities have been tried out with a wide age range of students. You may need to introduce them in a slightly different way for different age groups, but be prepared to take the risk and try them out. Where appropriate, variations are suggested for younger or older learners.

I believe that all students have a right to learn in safe, motivating, inclusive classrooms where differences are acknowledged and celebrated. Above all, teacher attitude is vital in making all students feel that they belong and are capable of learning. Students always remember how a teacher made them feel and a teacher who tried hard to understand them. This is more important than any technical knowledge you might feel you don't have.

I hope this book supports and inspires you in your teaching of students with SEN.

Part 1   General principles for SEN teaching

1   Introduction to SEN teaching

This chapter defines special educational needs (SEN) and discusses some of the key issues to consider when teaching students with SEN in the mainstream classroom.

What is SEN?

The term 'SEN' can have slightly different meanings in different parts of the world, and covers a wide range of student needs. In this book SEN is defined as follows:

> Students have special educational needs if they have significantly greater difficulty in learning than the majority of students of the same age and special educational provision has to be made for them.

In your country the definition of students with SEN might be slightly different. It might include, for example, students who have a different home language or students who come from disadvantaged backgrounds. You can find out what the current definition is from your school's SEN policy or from the Ministry of Education.

Ask yourself

Do you agree with this definition? Are there some students who are not covered by it?

The main categories of SEN are students with:
• cognition and learning needs
• communication and interaction difficulties
• **social, emotional, and behavioural difficulties (SEBD)**
• sensory impairments
• medical conditions.

(See Chapter 2 for more detail on each category.)

Some definitions of SEN include students who are **gifted and talented**, who need extra provision because they have significantly greater ability than their **peers**. We have included a chapter on these students in this book because they also need extra support from the teacher (see Chapter 13).

Students with SEN have wide-ranging and varied difficulties. Usually students with mild to moderate learning difficulties are included in mainstream schools. These students, and not those with more severe difficulties, are the focus of this book.

Inclusion

Many governments have introduced a policy of social and educational inclusion. Inclusion means giving all students a choice to be educated alongside their peers, irrespective of their individual needs and abilities.

In this book we have adopted the social model of inclusion. This model assumes that human differences are normal and that society must adapt to the needs of the person, rather than the person having to change to fit into society. The social model means we must work together to overcome barriers to learning for students with SEN, and adapt our teaching strategies and schools accordingly.

There is another view of inclusion, the medical model, whereby the student is seen as someone who has a problem that can be diagnosed, labelled, and treated. It is as if the student is 'faulty', and needs to be 'fixed'. Programmes and services are developed accordingly to help the students fit into society.

Ask yourself

- Which model operates in your country and in your school?
- What do you think are the advantages and disadvantages of each model?
- How would each model affect teaching plans?

To make lessons inclusive, teachers need to try and imagine what barriers prevent students with SEN from taking part in a particular lesson or activity. In your planning you should try and think of ways to remove or reduce those barriers so that all students can take part and learn. In some activities, students with SEN will be able to participate in the same way as the other students in the class. In others, you will have to adapt materials or tasks in order to include everyone.

Ask yourself

Imagine you have special educational needs, for example because you have **dyslexia**. What particular challenges do you think you would face in a school day?

Teacher attitude

Successful teachers of students with SEN tend to be flexible in their teaching approach and have a positive attitude. They are interested in their students and willing to learn from them. But it's not unusual for teachers to feel anxious about teaching students with SEN, especially if they haven't received any specialized training. The good news is that you don't need to be a specialist in psychology to teach students with SEN, because there are good, practical teaching strategies which you can use and which will benefit all your students. You do, however, need to be prepared to develop your teaching skills and to be aware of how your own beliefs and attitudes can affect interaction with students with SEN.

For example, 'labelling' students with SEN is unhelpful. Remember that every student is unique with his or her own personality. We don't assume, for example, that all students who wear glasses are the same. They can be introverts or extroverts – they aren't defined by their glasses – and the same applies to students with SEN. Make sure you see students with SEN as individuals, and get to know them, their interests and their strengths, as you would other students.

It is important to consider the language you use. Schools nowadays tend to use the terms special educational needs or **additional educational needs (AEN)**. In the past, a number of other terms were used to describe students with SEN, and you may have encountered some of them. They include:
- *mentally retarded, *defective, *handicapped
- *educationally subnormal.

However, in English these are now considered unacceptable and even offensive.

Ask yourself

What terminology is used in your L1 and that of your students? Does it matter which terms we use?

Dealing with bullying

Students with SEN can be vulnerable to bullying, particularly by students who don't know them personally. Systems need to be implemented to teach students to be aware of different needs and abilities. For example, you can introduce a 'buddy' system by asking a supportive peer to accompany students during break times if needed. Most importantly, you need to create a class ethos which values mutual support and understanding.

 **Getting it right**

Emphasize values

Introduce class rules which reinforce empathy and kindness to all students. Don't allow any laughing at other students. For example, say: *In this class we are kind and don't laugh at other people.* Praise students who demonstrate these values. For example, say: *I noticed Michael was really kind today.*

The inclusive classroom

Teaching and learning style

Do you teach in the same way as you like to learn? You will have students in your class who have very different learning styles from your own. Be curious, and learn from your students. You may find that some students are **visual learners**, so the use of visual aids would be appropriate to support their learning. Using games can work for many students with SEN as well as for those with no special needs. Many benefit from a multisensory approach.

Try this ☞ **See, hear, do**
Demonstrate grammar points physically and visually. Ask two students to hold a piece of string between them. Read out a sentence, for example: *She was eating her dinner, when the phone rang.* Get another student to touch the string in the middle to demonstrate the continuous aspect of the sentence. Finally draw the timeline in colour on the board.

✓ Getting it right

What works for them

Your students often know what helps them to learn more effectively. Don't be afraid to ask a student with SEN what works for them, and ask their parents/carers and other professionals too. Be prepared to try out a variety of activities which appeal to students with different learning styles (see Chapters 4, 6, and 7).

A supportive ethos

Teachers need to create a supportive, cooperative classroom atmosphere where all students feel noticed and valued. Inclusive classrooms are those where students help each other and celebrate their differences. You should set a good example when interacting with students with SEN and show that you respect the uniqueness of all your students. You can, for example, plan activities which encourage empathy, where students try to understand what life is like for someone else in the class.

Try this ☞ Similarities and differences

Ask students to work in pairs to find three things that they have in common and three things which are different. Ask them in feedback if anything surprised them. Encourage them to see that differences are also interesting.

Try this ☞ Guess about me

Ask students to work in pairs. Then ask four personal information questions. Students guess their partner's answers and write them down. Here's a sample question you could use: *What's your favourite colour/food/type of holiday?* Adapt the questions to your students' language levels and ages. Students show their guesses to their partner to see if they are correct.

Try this ☞ Make a presentation

Ask students if they would like to make a presentation to their classmates about their SEN and allow time in class for this. It can be in English or L1 depending on the age and level of your class. Check with their parents/carers that they are happy for this to happen.

Why this works ⫸

Developing empathy

Students often make judgements about each other which are wrong and lead to poor future interaction. Activities focusing on empathy allow students to gain insight into each other's worlds, developing their emotional skills and learning how easy it is to misjudge people. (See 'Self-esteem' in Chapter 3 and 'Social and emotional' in Chapter 10.)

Differentiation of work

Do you adapt or differentiate the tasks you assign to students so that they are achievable for everyone? Differentiation means adapting your plan and your teaching to take account of different student needs and abilities. All students will make progress in their learning, but in different ways. Work can be differentiated by task (different tasks for different abilities), content (adapted materials for different abilities), student response (students show understanding in different ways), self-access, or through extra one-to-one support. Differentiation is vital for teaching students with SEN (see Chapter 4).

Ask yourself

Do you think you differentiate for the different needs and abilities of your students? In what ways?

Classroom management

Teaching students with SEN isn't about learning a magic formula. Good classroom management and planning are essential in developing safe, inclusive classrooms. These are skills you probably already have. The tips below will benefit all learners but are particularly helpful for students with SEN.

1 Think carefully about where your students with SEN sit. Some students learn better by sitting near the teacher so they can see and hear instructions clearly. Others benefit from being seated away from windows or colourful wall displays which cause distraction or over-stimulation. Work with students to decide on the best place for them.

2 All students need structure and consistency to feel safe in the classroom, and this is particularly true of students with SEN. So make sure you have clear classroom rules. Remember that it's easier to start with clear rules and expectations than to try to establish them when students are misbehaving.

Try this ☞ **Class contract**

Ask students to write down five rules for the kind of class which they think would make learning safe and fun. Ask them to begin each rule with: *In this class, we …* (*listen to each other*, etc.). Then discuss which rules to use in the contract and put it up on your classroom wall. If students break the rules, use this as a learning opportunity to review the contract and the reasons for it.

Try this ☞ **Mini posters**

Allow students to have a mini poster of the rules on their desk as a reminder.

3 Clear instructions are essential for all students, but particularly important for those with SEN. Give an example of what you require and then get an example from your students to show they understand. Use gestures and visual aids to help students with SEN to understand and remember what to do. Use non-verbal routines to help reinforce instructions.

Try this ☞ **Visual support**

When giving instructions, use a non-verbal gesture to support the message – point to your ear or show a picture of an ear to indicate 'Listen'.

Try this ☞ **Traffic lights**

Use a traffic lights visual (with a movable arrow) to help with class discipline. Point the arrow to green when the class is on-task, point the arrow to orange when the group is going off-task and point the arrow to red when the group is off-task and needs to refocus.

4 Tell students what you want them to do, not what you don't want them to do. For example, say: *Look at the board* rather than *Don't turn round*. Talk about positive intentions behind inappropriate behaviours where possible. For example, say: *I know you want to tell me the answer, but I need you to put your hand up and wait* rather than *Stop calling out all the time and disrupting the class*.

5 Give students positive feedback on appropriate behaviour. Many students with SEN, particularly those with behavioural difficulties, only get noticed by the teacher for bad behaviour or when they make mistakes, which gives them no incentive to do the right thing.

6 Consider your body language and use of space in the classroom. Choose a place at the front of the class where you always stand to give instructions relating to tasks and another place for those relating to discipline – students will learn to associate different places with the type of instruction to expect.

Why this works ⫸

> **Structure**
>
> Clear and consistent classroom procedures, rules, and routines, combined with a positive attitude from the teacher, create a structured classroom environment that helps students to feel safe and secure. They know what is expected of them and are more likely to respond in the way you want them to.

2   Types of SEN

This chapter introduces the main categories of SEN and discusses the areas of difficulty each category typically covers (see Part 3 of the book for a detailed discussion of types of SEN).

The main categories of SEN

Cognition and learning

This category includes general learning difficulties and specific learning difficulties. Students with general learning difficulties make slower progress than other students in the same age group across all areas of learning. Students with specific learning difficulties, however, may only have problems in one area of learning – for example, reading and writing – and no problems in other areas.

General learning difficulties

For many students with general learning difficulties, the cause of their condition is not clear. Other conditions, such as **Down's syndrome**, are caused by genetic factors. These children usually have problems in many subjects and are behind their peers in literacy, numeracy, and general understanding. They might have problems with generalizing or with understanding abstract ideas. The degree of difficulty can range from mild to severe. Students with general learning difficulties might also have additional problems with motor skills (see Chapter 8), speech and language (see Chapter 12), working memory, and communication (see Chapter 3).

Try this ☞ **Checklists**

Create checklists to help students with longer tasks. Use pictures and words to guide the students, and use the same order of tasks wherever possible so that the checklists can be reused. This will help the students to develop good habits.

Try this ☞ **Start/Stop signals**

Have an agreed signal for starting and stopping an activity. For example, use a bell, a rattle, some music, or show a road sign.

 **Getting it right**

Peer learning

Students with general learning difficulties, particularly Down's syndrome, tend to copy the behaviour and attitudes of their peers. Encourage them to copy students who behave appropriately, and comment on students who are following the rules. For example, say: *Jada is waiting her turn. Can you do that too, Mina?* You can create (and name!) a team of peer supporters who will help students with general learning difficulties to remember rules and routines.

Specific learning difficulties (SpLD)

These students have problems with a specific area of learning, but are not necessarily behind their peers in other areas. Special educational needs in this category include dyslexia and **dyspraxia**. Some students may have more than one SpLD. Generally speaking, these learning difficulties affect students' motor skills, ability to process information, and memory (see Chapters 7 and 8).

Try this ☞ **Positive marking**

Use a marking system which allows you to give positive marks for good ideas and understanding. Don't always focus on correct grammar and spelling.

Try this ☞ **Walk my word**

Ask students to choose a word they find difficult to spell but want to remember. They should choose according to their own level. Ask students to write the word on a large piece of card, cut up the letters, put them on the floor and walk through the word, stepping on each letter in the right order.

 **Getting it right**

Little and often

Students will benefit from a very structured teaching approach which presents material little by little and often. So build in plenty of opportunities for practice and review to consolidate learning. This will help to develop a can-do attitude. And remember to praise students for any progress they make, however slow.

Communication and interaction

This category covers a wide range of problems such as disordered and delayed language skills, caused by different factors including developmental delay, sensory impairments, and severe speech and language disorders. Problems can range from mild to severe. This group includes students with **autism spectrum condition (ASC)**, such as **Asperger's syndrome**.

Speech and language difficulties (SLD) can be productive and/or receptive. These problems will often impact on a child's ability to learn another language. Students have problems with **productive language** when they have difficulty producing words and also making others understand what they are saying. They can also have difficulty finding words to express their thoughts, and may speak in short sentences using incorrect grammar or tense.

Students have problems with **receptive language** when they have difficulty understanding what another person is saying. They might be slow to respond to questions and instructions, or have limited vocabulary. Both students with ASC and those with speech and language difficulties can struggle to understand humour, and may have difficulties using language appropriately in social situations. It is vital to give these students more thinking time to understand information in class. Be patient when waiting for their answers and give them time to process your language. Remind other students of the rule: *We all wait quietly when someone needs time.*

✓ *Getting it right*

Attracting attention

Students need help in knowing when they should speak or listen in class. Teach students to be alert for stock instructions such as *Listen.* (Show a picture of an ear or point to your ear.) *Pens down, looking at me.* (Gesture.)

Always say the student's name before asking him or her a question.

Social, emotional, and behavioural difficulties (SEBD)

We use the term SEBD to describe a broad range of students with different needs, from those with emotional difficulties to those with very challenging behaviour or serious psychological difficulties. Teachers can find it difficult to know when a behaviour or range of behaviours represents a SEN and is not simply misbehaviour.

We use SEBD to describe problematic behaviour which:
- is severe
- isn't age appropriate
- happens frequently
- occurs in different situations.

The category includes students who are:
- disruptive
- challenging towards the teacher
- withdrawn
- impulsive
- hyperactive (students who have **attention deficit hyperactivity disorder (ADHD)**).

Students with SEBD and ADHD are often capable of learning another language if their behaviour can be managed in class.

Try this ☞ **Games for rules**

Play games such as 'Simon says' to show the importance of following rules. If the game goes wrong because of misbehaviour, stop and ask students why the rules are important. Elicit the idea that we can have fun and be safe if we have rules.

 **Getting it right** | **Focus on the positive**

Make your teaching and your attitude towards all students positive so that they feel valued and encouraged to behave and learn well. Establish clear guidelines for behaviour and keep the focus on learning. When you focus on a student's negative behaviour, it can be tiring for you and disruptive for the rest of the class. Stay in the learning zone, not the battle zone (see Chapter 10)!

Sensory impairments

This category covers a wide range of needs and abilities, including hearing, visual, or physical impairments. These disabilities are not covered in Part 3 of this book because they do not necessarily have an impact on a student's cognitive ability to learn a language. However, teachers may need to make adjustments to the learning environment; for example, the way furniture and seating is laid out. Make sure you consider any health and safety issues; for example, physical access to the school and classroom.

Getting it right | **See the person not the disability**

Talk to students about their disability and don't make assumptions – for example, that a visually impaired person can't see anything at all. Remember to see each student as an individual with her/his own strengths and weaknesses.

Medical conditions

Some children have medical conditions such as **asthma**, **anaphylaxis**, **diabetes**, and **epilepsy**, which need ongoing management and treatment. These conditions are not covered in Part 3 of this book. They shouldn't affect a student's ability to learn a language – although students may miss class due to illness, and this can affect their progress. Schools should keep a medical register containing information on student health issues. Make sure you know where the register is kept and what to do in a medical emergency.

Gifted and talented

Some definitions of SEN include students who are gifted and talented. This category covers students who have a particular talent or ability in one or more subjects. Students are considered gifted and talented when their ability is significantly greater than that of their peers, or if they show the potential to develop exceptional abilities.

Try this ☞ | **My twist**

Ask gifted and talented students to do the same activity as the rest of the class, but with a twist. For example, they could write a text for a specific audience, or as a certain character from a book.

 **Getting it right**

Challenge and stretch

Plan ways to challenge and stretch these students to keep them motivated. If they have a talent for languages, plan work with greater depth and breadth and allow opportunities for independent project work (see Chapters 4 and 13 for more ideas).

Identifying SEN

Some students are identified as having special needs due to their medical history. They may have been diagnosed with a genetic condition or a developmental disorder, or they may have sensory (visual, hearing, or physical) impairments. Other SEN are not so easy to identify. As a teacher, it isn't recommended that you try to diagnose SEN yourself. Students can struggle in class for a variety of reasons, and it's important to consider all factors which might be affecting their performance.

General indicators

Indicators that students might have difficulties greater than expected for their age and level include:
- having problems understanding and following instructions
- finding it difficult to concentrate and being easily distracted
- having difficulty with tasks which require fine or gross motor skills
- being able to speak much more fluently than they can write
- finding it difficult to start tasks or never managing to finish them
- avoiding doing tasks – for example, by arguing with the teacher
- having problems participating in whole-class or group activities
- appearing not to listen, or not responding to questions or instructions
- having problems making friends and maintaining relationships.

Remember that most students experience some of these difficulties from time to time. It's important to gather objective information about how often these problems occur and how serious they are. If you're concerned about a student in your class, discuss your concerns with other colleagues. If you discover they are having similar problems in all classes, discuss referring them to a specialist for a professional assessment and talk to their parents/carers, since they are usually the best people to give you advice about their child.

Observation checklist

You can use the checklist below to collect information about any student you are concerned about and to start making a support plan.

Checklist for teachers	Comments
Does the problem occur in every class and throughout the day?	
Does the problem occur only in certain class groupings?	
How is the student affected by the person they sit with?	
Can the student remember and follow instructions?	
Can the student work independently for longer periods of time?	
Is he or she easily distracted?	
Where does the student usually sit? Can they hear and see properly?	
Can the student wait their turn in class and group work? Can they interact and work well with other students?	
Does the student start/finish tasks on time?	
What types of tasks is the student good at and which does he or she actively enjoy?	
Does the student find activities too easy or too difficult? How do you know?	
Is the student able to ask for and accept help?	
Does the work involve a lot of writing? Sitting still? Copying from the board?	
Is there a noticeable difference between the student's spoken and written ability?	
Is the student only noticed for negative behaviour?	
Does the student have trouble remembering what to do?	

TABLE 2.1   *Observation checklist for teachers*

Why this works ▶

> **Overview of problems**
>
> Students might be having problems in class for many reasons. They might have difficulties in English but not in other school subjects. It's essential to get an overview of their problems in order to know how to proceed. By completing a checklist analysing their strengths and weaknesses in class, strategies can be put in place immediately to help them.

3 Common problem areas

As a classroom teacher, it isn't always possible and practical to use different strategies for different students. We try to see all our students as individuals, but in reality we often teach many classes and large numbers of students. Fortunately, it isn't necessary to have different strategies for each student. Remember that, when used effectively, strategies which help students with SEN should benefit the whole class. You can give general support to students with SEN by focusing on their common areas of difficulty. There are three areas in which most students with SEN, at some time and to some extent, have problems:

1 working memory
2 communication
3 self-esteem

Working memory

'Working memory' is a memory system which stores and works with information needed for everyday activities such as remembering phone numbers and following instructions. Problems with working memory in class can include difficulty in:

- following a sequence of instructions
- remembering things you've just read
- keeping your place in activities – for example, when reading or writing
- completing problem-solving activities.

Students who have difficulty with working memory might present certain behaviours in class such as not paying attention, daydreaming, or being easily distracted.

Try this ☞ **Number sequences**

2 7 1 4 3 9

Look at the numbers above, close your eyes, and try to remember them in sequence. After 30 seconds, try to write them down in the right order. Now look at them again, take 30 seconds to recall them in reverse order, and then write them down in reverse.

Ask yourself

Did you manage to recall all the numbers in ascending and descending order? How did you remember the numbers? Can you share your memory strategies with your students?

Improving working memory

Playing memory games can be a fun way of improving working memory. Memory games are particularly useful for remembering the spelling of words. Be careful, however, not to create more stress for students with SEN. Memory games can become very competitive, and students with SEN often compare themselves negatively with other students. Encourage students to share their memory strategies to help each other improve their memory.

Try this ☞ **My memory strategy**

Try the number sequences activity described on page 24 with your students. Ask them which numbers they managed to recall. Be careful not to ask: *Who got it right?* Ask a few students to explain how they remembered the number sequence in ascending and descending order. Do the activity again so students can try out different ways of remembering.

Try this ☞ **Word planes**

Ask a student to draw a plane on the board with a banner following it. Write a word in the banner and ask students to imagine the plane and the word in the air in front of them. Then rub both out. Can they still visualize the plane and the word? Once students are used to this idea, you can ask them to imagine and recall new words trailing behind a plane.

Try this ☞ **Mnemonics**

Make up sentences where each word begins with the letters of a difficult word, for example: ***b**ig **e**lephants **c**an't **a**lways **u**se **s**mall **e**xits* for 'because'. Encourage students to illustrate their sentences, as pictures can help to trigger memory too.

FIGURE 3.1   *Big elephants can't always use small exits*

Managing information

When you're presenting new information to the class, there are a number of things you can do to prevent overloading your students.

Use short sentences and simplify your instructions. If you're writing on the board, give students a written handout to refer to.

Present important information at the beginning of a lesson, and review it again at the end. Build in breaks and changes of focus throughout your lesson so that you create smaller endings and beginnings throughout the lesson.

Use verbal or visual prompts to help students remember important routines and instructions. Put a **visual timetable** of the day's routine on the wall (see Appendix 2, page 100). Use classroom lists to display the class rules, or word banks to display key vocabulary.

Try this ☞ **Personal prompts**

Ask students to write their own personal prompts to help them remember what to do. For example: *What do I need for this lesson? Who am I working with?*

Try this ☞ **Break it up**

Use a quick vocabulary game in the middle of a lesson to review key words before moving on.

Try this ☞ **Brain breaks**

Make a note of how long your class can concentrate for and build in a 'brain break' when you reach the limit. Students with SEN often feel that their brain is overloaded with information, and become anxious. They can give their brain a short break by:

- standing up and stretching
- doing a different task before returning to the previous one
- closing their eyes and resting their heads on the desk
- massaging their heads.

Encouraging independence

Students need encouragement to become more independent learners. With help they can develop their own learning strategies. You can discuss what works best for them, for example how best to organize their work using files, folders, highlighter pens, and colour-coding – or how to improve their listening by note-taking, drawing mind maps (see Appendix 3, page 101), or using a recording device.

Try this ☞ **My dictionary**

Encourage students to create their own glossaries or mini-dictionaries of key words and concepts they need to remember.

Try this ☞ **Memory cards**

Get your students to make memory cards of key language they need to review, with a question on one side and the answer on the other, for example. Students can use the cards to test themselves or get their classmates to test them.

Why this works ⫸

> **Independent learning skills**
>
> Developing strategies for independent learning early on will help students as they move from primary to secondary school, where they will be expected to work more independently.

Reading strategies

Students with poor working memory find reading comprehension activities difficult because they quickly forget information they have just read, saying that the words have 'fallen out of their heads'. They can easily become demotivated and end up abandoning tasks.

To prevent this, adapt reading texts to suit your students' interests and levels. For example, use shorter texts with illustrations which help with meaning. Use pre-reading tasks to encourage students to use their existing knowledge on the topic to begin reading with confidence.

Try this ☞ **Write your own short story**

Choose five or six keywords from the text. Ask students in pairs to make up a short story using these words. Students then read to see how their story compares with the real text.

Try this ☞ **Predict from titles**

Write the title of the reading text and any subtitles. Ask students in groups to predict what they think the text will be about before reading it.

Break texts up into chunks – or smaller parts – and include questions at different stages during the reading, not only at the end. The length of chunks can vary, depending on a student's reading level and the length of time they're able to concentrate for. Students can work in pairs or groups.

Try this ☞ **Highlight topic sentences**

Ask students to go through the text and highlight in one colour sentences at the beginning of paragraphs which explain what the paragraph is going to be about. Ask students to use another colour to highlight sentences at the end of paragraphs which summarize information.

Try this ☞ **Summarize**

Ask students to summarize the meaning of their chunk in ten words. This will help the teacher to check that they understand the gist. Alternatively, ask students to draw a picture which sums up the meaning.

Why this works ➡

Pre-reading tasks

Pre-reading tasks help to engage students and prepare them for the topic. Students with SEN often expect not to understand the text, so it's important to demonstrate to them that they can predict what they're going to read. Chunking helps students break down text into more manageable parts. It helps students identify key words and ideas, develops students' ability to summarize, and makes it easier for students to organize and process information.

Communication

Many students with SEN have difficulties with communication. This can affect their learning and their relationships with other children in their class. Communication difficulties will obviously show up in language classes, where listening, speaking, and interaction with peers have a high priority.

Listening

Students with SEN sometimes find it difficult to understand verbal communication, particularly long, complex instructions and speeches. They will need support in understanding what to do, and clear instructions are vital (see 'Classroom management' in Chapter 1). Try to build in activities which develop better listening skills for all students.

Try this 👉 **Checking instructions**

If you use numbers to rearrange students into groups, ask the students to say their number rather than you giving them numbers. Start by giving numbers to the first couple of students as an example, then ask students to carry on. When all students have a number, check they know them by saying *Number ones, put your hand up*, and so on. Then ask students to form groups according to their numbers.

Try this 👉 **Don't answer now**

Ask students to work in pairs. Student A asks Student B questions on a topic set by you and they begin when you say *Go*. Student B listens and tries to remember the questions without writing them down. Student B can only start answering the questions when you say *Stop*. Use this activity to practise tenses or other language points, according to the different age/level of your students.

Speaking

If students with SEN find it difficult to speak in their L1, they are going to find it even more challenging in an L2. Make sure you give them time to think, and the help they need to speak in class. Remember that pair and group work can help students too.

Try this 👉 **Think, pair, share**

When you ask the class a question:
- first give students two minutes to think
- then give them one minute to discuss ideas in pairs
- then ask pairs to share their ideas with the group/class.

This gives students time to process questions and think of a response.

Some students with SEN might understand an activity, and even have the right answer, but find it difficult to speak up in front of the whole class. They need different ways to show their understanding.

Try this ☞ **Mini whiteboards**

Students can write answers on their whiteboard and hold it up so the teacher can see. Students can also easily rub out a mistake if they get the wrong answer. (If you can't find mini whiteboards, laminate white A4 paper and use this as a wipe-off whiteboard.)

✓ *Getting it right*

Comprehension check

Mini whiteboards are a useful tool for the whole class. For example, you can use them to check comprehension quickly by getting all students to show you their answers on them.

Interaction with peers

Problems with communication can affect a student's interaction with their peers. Sometimes students can't understand humour, or use language in a way which other students find strange or rude. Whatever their problems, it's important for the teacher to plan opportunities for students to work together. As part of your lessons, you can encourage all students to think about their communication skills and the way they interact with each other in class.

Try this ☞ **My self-tracker**

Ask students to complete a checklist for themselves:

	☺	☹
How well did I do today?		
Listening to others		
Waiting my turn		
Speaking kindly		
Giving my opinion		
What do I need to do next time?		

TABLE 3.1 *Student self-tracker checklist*

Try this ☞ **Study buddies**

Use a system of 'study buddies' where students volunteer to help other students who are struggling to communicate in the classroom.

Try this ☞ **Shadowing and doubling**

In role plays, ask two students to share one role. One student stands behind their partner and helps them with language (by whispering in their ear to give encouragement or suggest new words). Or one student stands behind their partner and taps them on the shoulder when they want to take over.

Why this works ▥▶

Working together

When students work together, they can support and listen to each other. Students with communication difficulties can be involved in an activity without always having to speak themselves.

Self-esteem

The most important way a teacher can support students who are having difficulties is to build up their confidence and self-esteem. Students with SEN may have had experience of failing and making slow progress compared to other students. They can feel stupid, worthless, and even ashamed. As a result, students may appear anxious, demotivated, or uninterested in class.

Many students with SEN lack confidence in their abilities. It's important that you teach them ways to feel positive about learning. Make sure your attitude towards them is warm and positive. Smile, and be friendly and welcoming, even if you find the student challenging. Show you remember something about the student, such as the football team they support, or an interesting contribution they have made – and refer to it in the next class. This will help the student to feel important and valued.

Students can find it helpful to explain their SEN to the class if they're happy to do so (see page 15). They should never be forced to do this, but many students welcome the opportunity to talk about what it's like to be them, and what helps them in class.

Above all, focus on the student's strengths and interests. Students with SEN might not be good at reading and writing English, but they will have other abilities. Try to build on these. For example, if they're good at drawing, ask them to draw posters or charts for the classroom walls. Be aware that students with SEN are often trying really hard but aren't making much apparent progress.

Try this ☞   **Student of the week**

Reward students with a 'Student of the week' certificate for non-academic and personal qualities – for example, good social skills, sense of responsibility, perseverance, and kindness.

Try this ☞   **Thank you stars**

Ask students to write a positive comment about other students in the class on one side of a piece of paper and draw a star on the other side. Stars can be given out at any time – they should help students to appreciate each others' good qualities.

Try this ☞   **Imaginary wristbands**

Ask students to think about a time when they felt really happy and confident; for example, on holiday, playing a sport, or doing something they love. Now tell the students to hold their wrists and imagine putting that great feeling onto an imaginary wristband. They can then touch their imaginary wristband any time they need to feel confident.

Part 2   Ways of working to address SEN

4　Differentiated teaching

> I know about the need to differentiate in class, but to be honest it takes a long time to adapt worksheets for different students and I don't know how to do it more effectively.
>
> JORGE, SECONDARY TEACHER, BRAZIL

Differentiated teaching is when we plan and structure lessons to take account of all students in the class, whatever their individual level and abilities. The goal is for all students to make progress in their learning, whatever their starting point. Some activities can be done in the same way by all students. But other activities will need to be adapted, and you may need to provide parallel activities in order to include everyone.

Like Jorge, as teachers you are probably aware of the need to differentiate work for students so that they can work at their own pace and learn successfully. There are many ways you might already differentiate; for example, moving a child who has problems copying words down to be seated near the front of the class, or giving an early finisher an extra task. Differentiation simply means acknowledging that students are individuals who learn in different ways and at different rates.

Ask yourself

How do you currently differentiate work in your classes? Do you find that differentiation is very time-consuming?

Know your students

Differentiation starts with getting to know your students as individuals. You need to know their preferred learning environment. Do they need to sit away from distractions? Do they need to work with a peer? What is their preferred learning style (visual, auditory, **kinaesthetic**)? What are their areas of interest (e.g. art, football, music)?

You can get to know your students through simple language activities.

Try this ☞ **Register game**
Build opportunities to get to know your students into your normal class routines. When you call the register, ask students to answer with their favourite colour, food, or favourite word from the week.

Try this ☞ **'Me' posters**

Ask students to make a 'Me' poster including information about their family, interests, holidays, and likes or dislikes. Students talk about their posters together in small groups. Give students opportunities to add to the posters over the course of the year as they get to know each other better.

Ways to differentiate work

Most classrooms are mixed-ability, and teachers are used to dealing with this in various ways, such as deciding how to pace a lesson so students don't get bored or overwhelmed – or by ensuring that instructions to the class are clear and simple so that everyone understands. But there are also some key ways we can differentiate by:

- task
- content
- student response
- self-access materials
- extra one-to-one support from a teaching assistant (see page 44 for more on this)
- assessment.

Differentiate by task

Differentiation by task means setting different tasks to match the abilities of your students. You don't, therefore, need to prepare different content for different groups. You could, for example, either produce two or more worksheets at different levels, or one worksheet where the questions become progressively more challenging.

Try this ☞ **Dictation**

Dictate a short text to the whole class, but vary the task for different groups. The first group listens and writes down the whole text. The second group completes a gapped text. The third group completes the same gapped text, but chooses answers from multiple-choice options.

Try this ☞ **Vocabulary**

Give the whole class the same word search, but give different instructions to different groups. Tell some students how many words to find. Support others by giving pictures for each word. For more support, provide a full list of the target words for some students.

Try this ☞ **Storytelling**

Tell the students a story. Ask some students to retell the story from picture prompts and others to retell the story by putting key sentences from the story in the right order.

Why this works ⫸

> **Save time**
>
> It's less time-consuming for the teacher to change the task than to change the content. It's also motivating for students with SEN to see that they are working with the same content as other students and focusing on the same language point.

Questions

Some students will need simple questions and some students will be able to cope with more complex questions. Factual questions are generally easier for students to answer than abstract questions. Questions which require imagination, analysis, and inference are more complex for students to answer.

1 Closed questions have only one correct answer. They include Yes/No questions, True/False questions, and multiple-choice questions.
2 Open-ended questions have more than one possible answer and allow the student more choice. They include questions like: *How do you … ? What do you think about … ?*

Ask yourself

Which question is easier to answer? Why?
1 How many stepsisters does Cinderella have?
2 How do you think Cinderella feels towards her stepsisters?

Try this ☞ **Questions bank**

Create a bank of questions which range in difficulty from factual and closed to open-ended and imaginative, and try them out with your next class. Notice which students respond best to each type of question.

 **Getting it right**

> **Match questions to students**
>
> Some students such as those with autism spectrum condition (ASC) or speech and language difficulties will benefit from being asked fact-based closed questions. They need to feel confident with answering these questions before moving on to more complex questions. Gifted students will benefit from open-ended questions which allow for freer expression. Also, be aware that some students are able to answer complex spoken questions but find written questions more difficult, whereas other students find writing easier than speaking.

Differentiate by content

Differentiation by content means adapting the content of a task, for example a reading text. Students can be given slightly different texts and asked to find out the same information. This allows them to work at their own level and complete the same task. A text can be made slightly easier with short factual sentences, or slightly more complex with longer sentences and sub-clauses. Students can choose which text to read.

Try this ☞ **What colour do I feel like today?**

Create colour-coded worksheets with graded content, but focusing on the same task. Allow students to choose which colour they want to work on, as this may help to remove the potential stigma of different colours denoting lower and higher ability. If you notice that some students always choose one that is too easy or too difficult, encourage them to choose another colour more appropriate for their level.

✓ **Getting it right**

Return on investment of time

Think about the return on investment of your time and make sure that you create materials which you can use again with other classes. Aim to create a bank of reusable resources rather than a series of 'one use only' materials.

Differentiate by student response

Differentiation by response means allowing students to respond to activities and tasks in different ways and according to their level of ability.

Different ways of responding

When teachers set tasks, they don't expect one single 'right' answer or one particular style of response (e.g. spoken).

Try this ☞ **Football cards**

Students hold up a coloured card to indicate whether they understand a point or not.

Red card = I don't understand it.

Yellow card = I understand some of it.

White card = I understand all of it.

Try this ☞ **ABCD cards**

Make cards with a different letter on each one: A, B, C, and D. When you want to check understanding, read out four versions (A to D) of the target language and ask students to hold up the card for the correct version. Students can work on their own or in pairs/small groups. For example:

    A I have lived here since four years.

    B I lived here since four years.

    C I have lived here for four years.

    D I live here for four years.

This can be done via an electronic voting system if your class uses tablets.

Try this ☞ **Language review**

Ask students to summarize a key topic or language point using their preferred learning style (visual, auditory or kinaesthetic).

Visual: a poster, a cartoon, stick figures and speech bubbles, a mind map (see Appendix 3, page 101)

Auditory: a song, a rhyme, an interview, a radio play

Kinaesthetic: a game, a role play, a 3D model

Allow students to decide which group they want to work in. Give them time to prepare their presentation and present it to the class.

Try this 👉 **Word stress**

Practise word stress using different learning styles.

Visual: students mark dots representing the stress of the syllables:
giraffe ●●   hippopotamus ●●●●●

Auditory: students sing or hum the stress, using a higher note or louder hum for stressed syllables.

Kinaesthetic: students walk the stress around the room, taking a long step for stressed syllables and a short step for unstressed syllables. For example: hippopotamus = short step, short step, long step, short step, short step.

✓ *Getting it right*

Play to their strengths

Every student has a preferred learning style, so play to his or her strengths. Students who find it hard to speak in front of the class may be happier to present their learning in writing. Others will prefer to present their learning in pictures. Some students will benefit from being allowed to demonstrate their learning physically, for example, through role play or music.

Different levels of response

Open-ended activities allow students to give different responses according to their level of ability.

Try this 👉 **Find someone who ...**

Write the first three questions using the language point you want to practise, and then ask students to add three more (encourage stronger students to write as many as they can in the time available). Students walk around the class and ask each other their questions, noting down the names of students who say 'yes'.

> **Find someone who ...**
>
> 1 can swim: _____
>
> 2 can run fast: _____
>
> 3 can play tennis: _____
>
> 4 _____ : _____
>
> 5 _____ : _____
>
> 6 _____ : _____

FIGURE 4.1   *Student 'Find someone who ...' questionnaire*

Ask yourself

Which tasks in your lesson plans for next week could you hand over to students to write?

Different levels of responsibility

It's important to give jobs and responsibilities to students who are not usually trusted by the teacher to do them – perhaps because they are not necessarily the highest achievers or best-behaved students. Give out jobs according to the needs of your students; for example, students who find it hard to sit still could be given the responsibility of walking around and collecting books.

Try this ☞ **Class monitors**

Allocate classroom jobs to different students in the class. Jobs could include giving out work or equipment, writing the date on the board, or organizing moving tables for mingling activities.

Try this ☞ **Noise monitors**

Choose a monitor to keep track of noise levels during class. Use cards to signal noise levels – a card with a frowning face (too noisy), a neutral expression (acceptable), and a smiling face (good) – during group or pair work.

Try this ☞ **Self-marking**

Ask students to use your **marking criteria** to check their own work. Encourage them to set their own learning targets based on the results of their self-marking.

Try this ☞ **Definitions**

Ask abler students to write definitions of keywords from a topic and to put them on the class word wall. Encourage them to write the definitions in a way which helps all students understand.

Why this works ⫸

> **Responsibility for all students**
>
> Students with SEN benefit from being given responsibility because it helps them feel included and valued. It can also help improve the attitude of students with poor behaviour. But giving abler students more responsibility for their learning can also be motivating and good for self-esteem, especially for shy or less confident students. (See Chapter 13 for more ideas).

Differentiate by self-access activities

Another way to differentiate is to create time in your lessons when students work independently on self-access materials. This requires some organization by the teacher, but over time you can build up materials for use during self-access time. If the class can work on computers, there are even more opportunities available for students to work on individual programs (see Chapter 6).

Try this ☞ **Graded readers**

Build regular reading time into your lessons by using graded readers. Try and build up a collection of readers about similar topics with different word levels. Then your students can sometimes discuss the same topics as each other and read together at their own level.

Try this ☞ **Graded comprehension cards**

Create reading comprehension cards based on your class reader. Colour-code the questions so that all students can engage with the same topic at their own level.

Try this ☞ **Extension activities**

Prepare a list of activities which students can work on if they finish early. For example:

- stories – change the ending
- topics – do further research online and find out some facts the class doesn't know
- vocabulary – add ten more words to the topic.

✓ *Getting it right*

Small steps

It can be difficult to know where to start with differentiation. You don't need to begin by differentiating every lesson. Start with a small, realistic target; for example, plan to differentiate two lessons in a week. Or focus on two different students each week, planning activities for them, so that eventually you include everyone.

Differentiate by assessment

It might also be necessary to differentiate in the way you assess students. Assessment can be frustrating for students with SEN. They won't necessarily be able to achieve at the same level or in the same way as their peers. They might, for example, need more time to write answers in exams, or they might need help in reading the questions. They can easily get demotivated if they are always assessed in comparison to their peers. It is important to use different ways to check understanding (see 'Different ways of responding' on page 35) and allow students to show what they know. One way to include more motivating assessment experiences is to use 'assessment for learning' (AfL).

Assessment for Learning

Traditional 'assessment of learning' (AoL) involves teacher-designed and marked tests, which assess performance at the end of a unit or period of study. Students receive marks and can compare themselves with others in the class. AfL, on the other hand, involves students assessing and managing their own learning at their own pace. The teacher works with students to identify what they already know, and then encourages them to take an active part in setting their own targets and assessing their own progress. AfL is ongoing and occurs at all stages of a lesson and school year. It can help students with SEN because it allows them to measure their progress against their own achievable goals and not against the results of others. Teachers use marking systems which give students clear criteria on what they have done well and how to improve on their own targets next time.

Try this ☞ **Two stars and a wish**

When you mark homework, give students two comments which are positive (two stars) and one comment which gives them something to improve on (a wish).

Try this ☞ **Ladders**

Use a graded system, visualized as a ladder, to represent the steps to achieving a target. Students can colour in the rungs of the ladder as they make progress.

Try this ☞ **The KWL grid**

Give students the title and a brief explanation of the topic that they will be working on. Ask them to work on a KWL grid (**K**now, **W**hat, **L**earned). They should fill in the first two columns before they have studied the topic and the third at the end of the topic.

K What I know or think I know	W What I want to know	L What I have learned

TABLE 4.1   *The KWL grid*

Why this works ⏩

> **Measure your own progress**
>
> It is very demoralizing to always get poor marks in tests, and students automatically compare their results with those of their peers. Assessment for Learning (AfL) allows them to see and measure their own progress and to feel that they are moving forward.

Formal assessments

In most school systems students with SEN still have to undergo formal assessments of learning. Find out what allowances can be made for students in official examinations; for example, if they can have extra time in examinations, receive help from a **scribe**, use a laptop, take the examination in a smaller room with fewer people around, or record their answers in a different format, such as an audio recording.

5   Working collaboratively

> I wish I knew how to deal with David's parents. They constantly want to meet me to talk about their son. I don't think they believe I'm teaching him properly.
>
> EVA, SECONDARY TEACHER, HUNGARY

Do you ever feel like this when meeting the parents/carers of students with SEN? It isn't unusual. Teachers are rarely given training in how to communicate effectively with parents/carers who have often had to fight for their child's rights. They can come across as combative and challenging. However, they can be your best ally if you create a good relationship with them. They know their child best and will have helpful suggestions to make. It's also important to work with other professionals and agencies who can support your teaching of students with SEN and offer valuable strategies and advice. In this chapter we will look at the best ways to work with parents/carers and professionals to ensure students with SEN achieve their potential.

Acceptance of SEN

Some parents/carers, for personal or cultural reasons, find it difficult to accept that their child might have SEN. Be respectful of their feelings and listen to their concerns. Remember that teachers are not qualified to give diagnoses. You can collect information using the checklist in Chapter 2 (see page 23) and try to find out as much as possible about the student's needs. After this, you might decide to ask an **educational psychologist** for more help and assessment.

You must involve the parent/carer in your assessment of the student's needs, and be very careful when discussing this sensitive issue with them. Focus on explaining the problems you see the student experiencing in class and ask if they have noticed similar issues at home, for example when doing homework. Frame the interventions as a positive step forward and empathize with their feelings. You could say, for example: *I understand that this is worrying, but I can see John is trying very hard and would like to find ways to support him more.*

Objections from other parents/carers

Some parents/carers of other students might be concerned that their child is in a class with a student with SEN. They may worry that their own child won't make good progress if the teacher is focusing on the needs of the student with SEN. It's important that you plan how to deal with these questions.

These parents/carers want reassurance from you as the teacher. Acknowledge their anxiety and assure them that their child is not being overlooked. They may not be convinced of the benefits of inclusion, but they will often take their lead from you. You will need to explain the benefits and always give them clear feedback on their own child's progress so that they know their child's needs are being met.

✓ *Getting it right*

Promoting inclusion

Emphasize that all students benefit from learning in inclusive classrooms because they will learn to value diversity and develop empathy and teamwork skills, all of which are recognized nowadays as vital for success in life and work. Encourage parents/carers to see that inclusive classrooms help develop students into valuable members of society.

Working with parents/carers

For busy teachers, liaising with families can seem complex and time-consuming. However, in the long term it often saves time and reduces frustration by giving the school important insights into the best ways to support students. Good communication between home and school is vital. It ensures that ideas can be shared and situations dealt with as soon as they arise.

When a student has ongoing problems in various classes, teachers need to decide who will keep in contact with parents/carers, because it can create conflict and anxiety if several different teachers contact them at different times.

Discuss a way of keeping in contact which suits you and the parents/carers. This might be via email or phone calls. It is better to set a regular time and way of communicating, rather than only contacting the parents/carers when a problem arises. This way you can provide positive as well as negative feedback.

✓ *Getting it right*

Nominated teacher contact

Suggest to your school that you establish a system for recording feedback and comments on students with SEN. Choose one member of staff to give regular feedback to parents/carers.

Try this  **Home–school notebook/diary**

Use a home–school notebook/diary for parents/carers and teachers to share important information and feedback.

Try this  **Praise postcards**

Create or buy a set of postcards with positive pictures on them. Try to send a positive message to parents/carers on the postcards throughout the school year. Focus on something specific, such as progress made in speaking or listening.

Positive language

Be careful about using negative language when talking to parents/carers about their child. Describe the student's behaviour and separate this from your judgement of the student.

Don't say: *Your son is very lazy.*

This is a negative start to a discussion.

Do say: *Your son finds it difficult to finish work on time, and I often notice that he is looking out of the window.*

This describes the student's behaviour and is non-judgemental in tone. It's a good starting point for having a constructive conversation about finding possible solutions to address the problem. Also, be sure to use inclusive language to emphasize the fact that you're working in partnership. For example, say 'we' rather than 'you' and 'I'.

 *Getting it right*

Open-ended questions

Use open-ended questions in meetings with parents/carers when you want to involve them and get their opinions. For example, ask:
How ... (can we work together on this)?
Can you tell me about ... ?
Avoid starting questions with 'Why', because this can make listeners feel defensive.

Ask yourself

Think about the last time you talked with the parents/carers of a student with SEN. What worked well and what didn't work so well? How could you improve your approach?

Defusing conflict

When disagreements arise, use strategies to defuse potential conflicts:
• Listen carefully to parents/carers
• Speak calmly and politely
• Acknowledge angry or negative feelings by saying: *I can understand you're disappointed and upset at the moment.*

Always try to identify a positive intention in their comments and reactions. Remember that they just want the best for their child. Keep the focus of the discussion on the student's learning needs. Questions from parents/carers don't mean they disagree with your authority; choose to believe that they're trying to clarify a situation and be helpful, rather than telling you how to do your job.

 *Getting it right*

Stack up 'yes' responses

Begin any potentially difficult conversation by making a series of statements in quick succession which you know parents/carers will agree with. This immediately shows empathy. For example:
I know you're very busy and you've taken time off work because you want to get this sorted out.
You want the best for your child, and we do too.

A whole-school plan

Your school should have an action plan for any student with SEN in your school. This plan needs to be created in meetings with parents/carers, the student, and other adults who are involved in support. The plan needs to be reviewed regularly with parents/carers.

This plan should include information about:
- the student's strengths and areas of difficulty
- the short-term targets set for or by the student
- the teaching strategies to be used
- the student's and parents'/carers' views
- any extra support to be put in place
- the person responsible for monitoring and reviewing the targets
- the date for reviewing the plan
- success and/or exit criteria.

Plans for students with SEN need to be practical documents, not unworkable documents which stay unread in an office file. Keep them short and make sure all members of staff know the targets and strategies. Try to accommodate parents/carers with regard to the time of meetings, and set up meetings well in advance. If parents/carers can't attend, check if another family member is able to attend and represent their views. Consider the best place to hold the meeting; formal offices can sometimes be intimidating for parents and carers.

Ask yourself

Where are your meetings usually held? Do you sit behind your desk? If so, how does this make parents/carers feel? How can you put parents/carers at ease?

Working with other professionals

It is important to be aware of other professionals who can help you in working with students with SEN. Some of the people who might work at your school or in your district include:
- **speech and language therapists**
- educational psychologists
- resource/specialist SEN teachers and advisors
- **occupational therapists**
- staff from specialist charities/**NGOs**.

 **Getting it right**

Support agencies

Compile a list of people who can give extra help and support to students with SEN. You can search on Google for local support, and your head teacher should also know what the local education services can offer. Check out their resources and training.

Teaching assistants/helpers

Some teachers have teaching assistants working in their class to support students with SEN. If you do, it's important to plan and work together to make the best use of their help. When funding isn't available for teaching assistants, some teachers find ways to bring local adults into the school to help them. These adults can be retired teachers, students on work experience, or even parents/carers. The teacher remains responsible for the student's learning, but these assistants can provide valuable support. They can work on a more individual basis with students who need extra support.

Teaching assistants/helpers can:

- sit next to students and check that they understand what to do
- act as a reader or scribe for students with reading/writing difficulties
- talk through an exercise before students write down ideas, helping to organize their thoughts
- encourage students to speak up and answer in class
- take note of students' strengths, interests, and special talents, and feed back to the teacher to help in planning
- help arrange groups for group work and go around checking students know what to do
- go around the class checking students are on track, giving instant feedback on behaviour and performance.

Ask yourself

Do you think it's a good idea to bring volunteers into your class? What are the advantages and disadvantages?

You will need to think carefully about how to use extra help in your class. Draw up a plan with your assistant and write down strategies to use with certain students. Make sure you both have a copy of the plan. Be clear about your different roles and try to meet regularly to give feedback. In your lesson plans, write down how you will use the teaching assistant and what they need to do. Make sure any assistants have an induction into the school and are aware of policies and safety procedures.

 *Getting it right*

Planning

Decide on a system of communication. For example, use a daybook to record any important messages, make good use of a staff noticeboard, use email, and make sure staff minutes are circulated to everyone. Make sure there is a written record of important points. Encourage the teaching assistants to attend training.

6 Assistive technology
Sally Farley

What is assistive technology?

Assistive technology (AT) is a broad term which covers computer software and apps as well as devices and equipment designed or adapted to help people with a wide range of SEN and disabilities. It includes everything from pencil grips that help a child write more easily to hearing aids or programs that read text aloud from the computer screen. AT allows people with SEN and disabilities to do things that would be impossible for them to do without it, and it can make a real difference to students. It gives them tools to work more independently, and can help them overcome barriers to learning. In the English class, AT can help with reading and writing, organization, motivation, and working memory. It can be invaluable to learners with visual and hearing impairments, as well as those with other physical and coordination difficulties.

The right AT programs and tools can help students with SEN:
- gain confidence and build self-esteem
- improve literacy
- work independently
- show what they know
- overcome frustration and tiredness.

This chapter will look at ways in which AT can help you to create a more inclusive classroom.

 **Getting it right**

> **Free software**
>
> Assistive technology need not be costly, and many accessibility features are already built into most computers. There's also lots of helpful software available on the internet which is completely free to download and use. If you are searching for free software, it helps to use the words 'open source' and 'freeware' in your search.

Reading support

Text to speech

Nearly all computers come with a built-in voice which can be used to read out text from the screen. Although these 'voices' lack the intonation and expression of natural speech, they can be a great help to students who read hesitantly and find it difficult to concentrate on text. It can be hard for a student to understand the meaning of a text when they get 'stuck' on certain words, and screen readers can overcome this problem by reading fluently. Some text-to-speech software highlights the words as it reads them, helping students to focus their attention on the text as they listen. Different programs can be used to read documents that have been scanned into the computer, for example from e-books and web pages as well as students' own work.

Try this ☞

Speak button

You can make Microsoft Word (2010 version and newer) read out text by adding a 'Speak' button to the Word toolbar. For students (and teachers!) who find written instructions confusing, there are videos explaining how to do this on YouTube. Once the 'Speak' button is added, students can use it to read back their own work, helping them to spot mistakes and also improve their writing style.

Learning to read

Students with SEN, particularly those with dyslexia, often have trouble learning to read. AT can help with all stages of reading, from learning the alphabet and linking letters to sounds to reading words by **segmenting** and **blending** phonemes. There are many programs designed to improve phoneme identification and awareness. Students can use games and puzzles to learn familiar sounds and word families, manipulate letters to make words, and practise rhyming, blending, and **chunking** skills. These programs can be really helpful for students learning English, as they introduce the complexities of English spelling systematically through activities that are enjoyable and rewarding. High-frequency words can be repeated and practised in different ways until they enter long-term memory. These features are especially helpful for students with dyslexia and other reading difficulties, as they allow them to work at their own pace, build confidence, and increase their motivation to read.

Online resources for learning reading and spelling in English

'Teach Your Monster to Read' is a free game that allows students to develop and practise skills for the first stages of reading (see *Useful websites*).

In the game, students explore an imaginary world and complete a series of challenges which help them (and their pet monster!) to read. They can develop their listening skills and learn English pronunciation by matching letters to sounds. They also practise blending and segmenting phonemes.

Wordshark is a commercial teaching resource that has over 50 games through which students can learn and practise literacy skills (see *Useful websites*). Each game focuses on a particular aspect of reading and spelling and has different levels and speeds, giving scores and timings each time it is played. The teacher options allow you to set up work plans for individual students and monitor their progress. Students who like challenges and enjoy working quickly can play against each other.

Visual stress and tracking difficulties

Some learners see words as blurred or moving on the page or screen. This can be the result of 'visual stress', which is caused by the stark contrast of black text on a white background. Changing the background colour of the screen and/or the colour of the font can be a simple way of solving the problem. Some readers have difficulty tracking or keeping their eyes fixed on the text, which means they keep losing their place. This can be helped by using a program which highlights individual words or lines as they are read.

Try this ☞ **Coloured screen overlay**

T-Bar is a coloured screen overlay which is available free from www.eduapps.org. The product is available in a range of colours. Show students how to experiment with different colour backgrounds and fonts until they find the combination which is easiest for them to read.

Teens talk about money!

'**My pocket money** (*paghetta*) **is £30 a month.** My brother gets £40 every month, but he's older than me. I have to get good **marks** (*voti*) at school and I also have to do some housework for my pocket money. I have to take the dog for a walk, do the washing up and tidy my bedroom. I like taking the dog for a walk, but I hate doing the washing up. It's the most boring job in the world!

I spend my pocket money on cinema tickets, snacks and mobile phone credit! The most expensive thing is my phone. I spend £15 a month on phone credit, but I can't live without my phone!

My parents pay for my clothes, school things and transport. I take the train to school and I have a student **travel card** (*tessera di abbonamento*). When I want something special I have to save for it. Last year I saved £60 and I bought an MP3 player.' **Holly**

'**I get £6.50 pocket money every week.** To get my pocket money I have to work hard at school and I have to help my mum with the housework. I have to tidy my room and load and unload the dishwasher. When I don't help Mum, she only gives me £5 for the week! At the weekend, I visit my grandma and she usually gives me some money. I always get money for my birthday and at

FIGURE 6.1   *Coloured screen overlay (Text from* High Five Testmaker for Students with Dyslexia, *Oxford University Press 2014)*

Speed-reading software

Students with SEN are often slow and hesitant readers. Speed-reading software can sometimes help them to improve their reading speed and fluency, as they only see one word on the screen at a time. This reduces eye strain and the need to 'stay on track' as they read a paragraph of text. It may not work for all students, but it's free and easy to try.

Try this ☞ **Speed-reading plug-in**

You can try speed-reading at www.spritzinc.com. If you or your students find it helpful, you can install Spritzlet, which is a free plug-in that works with your web browser. Once it's installed it's simple to use (follow the instructions provided on the website).

Writing support

Voice recognition software

Voice recognition software converts spoken words into text. It's a helpful tool for students who are good at expressing their thoughts and ideas verbally but have difficulty writing them down. It allows students to dictate their ideas freely, without having to stop and think about spelling. It's useful for students with dyspraxia or other coordination difficulties because they don't need handwriting or typing skills. They can also control the computer without using a mouse or keyboard, by giving voice commands. Speech recognition is built into Windows and can be set up by going through 'Control Panel' to the list of 'Ease of Access' options.

✓ *Getting it right*

Train the computer

Before you can use a voice recognition program, the computer must get to know the user's way of speaking. It does this by asking the user to read out a text that appears on the screen. This can be hard for students with reading difficulties, as the text needs to be read accurately and fluently. Help students by printing out the text and practising it with them until they feel confident about 'training' the computer. Some students will enjoy dictating their ideas and others may not, so let them decide for themselves whether to do it.

Try this ☞ **Print out key commands**

If a student wants to use voice commands to control the computer, search 'voice recognition' in Windows Help and Support for a tutorial that you can go through together. Find the key commands and print them out.

Touch-typing

Learning to touch-type is an important skill, especially for learners with poor handwriting. It makes their work legible and helps them to write more quickly. Touch-typing helps learners with working memory difficulties, as they don't have to keep shifting their attention from the keyboard to the screen. Touch-typing also helps learners with spelling difficulties, because it gives them a kinaesthetic way of remembering common letter patterns like 'tion' or 'the'.

There are several free touch-typing tools available online (see 'Portable applications' on page 51). Dance Mat Typing is a colourful, fun version for primary students (see *Useful websites*).

Planning and organizing support

Students with SEN often have trouble organizing their thoughts and sequencing ideas. Graphic organizers can make a big difference to all kinds of writing and learning tasks. They appeal to visual learners and work by breaking down information and ideas into smaller, more manageable steps. They can be used for structuring writing, problem-solving, planning, and making decisions. Examples and downloadable templates can be found at: www.eduplace.com.

Mind mapping software

Mind maps are perfect for **holistic thinkers**, as they give an overview or 'big picture' of the subject (see Appendix 3, page 101). They are also a useful tool for brainstorming and getting ideas down very quickly. Students can include images, notes, and hyperlinks under their different topics. Mind maps help them to plan, add, and sort ideas using key words, images, and colour to make the information easier to process and remember. If necessary, they can convert their ideas into the linear format required for essay writing and answering exam questions.

Managing time

Students with SEN can find measuring and organizing time difficult. Timers, available on tablets, can be used as visual aids to show how much time is left to finish an activity. They can also help students who have difficulty moving from task to task by preparing them for the transitions.

Memory support

Often students with SEN have problems remembering things. They forget appointments, instructions, and directions, and lose school books and other important items. They have difficulty remembering facts, such as important dates or new vocabulary. AT can help and, once students become familiar with the different applications available, they can use them to support memory in all areas of their lives.

Try this ☞ **Online diary**

If you have students who are constantly late, lose or forget their homework, and are generally disorganized, you can encourage them to use an online diary. This gives them an overview of the day/week/month and allows them to colour-code information, and add tasks, projects, and appointments. Students can set alarms to remind them well in advance. The Sunbird Calendar is included in MyStudyBar (see 'Portable applications' on page 51), and there are many other free online calendars available on the internet, including one from Google.

FIGURE 6.2   *Electronic calendar*

Remembering words and facts

A good way to remember new language is to link it to things you already know. These associations can be made in multisensory ways that involve imagination, emotion, and enjoyment. In order for the new information to be stored in the long-term memory, the learning needs to be reinforced through repeated testing and reviewing. Students with SEN may need to **overlearn** and revisit new information more often than others, and AT provides a way to do this which is effective, enjoyable, and often completely free.

Try this ☞   **Memrise.com**

This website is helpful for learning vocabulary (see *Useful websites*). Each new word is spoken and accompanied by a choice of memory aids that include pictures, mnemonics, photos, videos, etymologies, and example sentences. Learners choose the one they find most memorable and appealing, and this is repeated every time the word is used.

Try this ☞   **Quizlet.com**

This website allows learners to download flashcards to their computer or mobile phone (see *Useful websites*). This is a really effective way for visual learners to memorize English vocabulary, because they can flick through the cards whenever they have a few spare minutes. They can go to the website and find appropriate study tools to practise language learning, including multiple choice and other types of quizzes. **Auditory learners** can record their own voice on the website, or listen to text-to-speech audio recorded by native speakers.

Try this 👉 **Using tablets to record and revise information**

Taking photos is a good way of recording and remembering information if students have difficulty copying from the board. Videos can also be used. If you're explaining a particular point, encourage the students to record the explanation on a tablet so that they can listen to it again later.

Portable applications

Portable applications can be loaded on to USB sticks (pen drive) and used on any computer, which means students can use them wherever they go.

Try this 👉 **MyStudyBar**

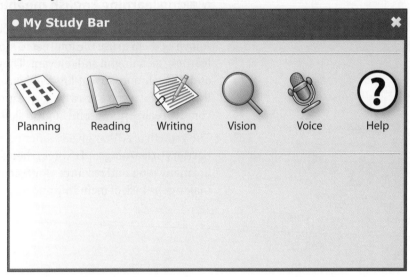

FIGURE 6.3   *Screenshot of* MyStudyBar (v3)

MyStudyBar is a free 'floating' toolbar to support literacy, available at www.eduapps.org. It includes mind mapping software, **screen masking**, word prediction, voice recognition, diary and planner in the form of a portable calendar, text-to-speech functionality, a talking dictionary, and more. Introduce students to it and let them use the applications they find most helpful.

AT and ASC

Working on a computer can provide a safe alternative for learners with ASC who find working in groups stressful. It also offers the chance to experience the world 'virtually', through multimedia programs and the internet. Students with ASC can learn about the world and practise living and working in it within the controlled environment of the computer.

Try this 👉 **Social skills**

Kar2ouche is a piece of educational software that allows you to create video scenarios of social situations which students with ASC can interact with (see *Useful websites*). This allows them to rehearse appropriate ways of responding in groups, such as turn-taking, sharing, listening, and empathizing with others.

 *Getting it right*

Technology in moderation

Although AT can provide a refuge from the sensory overload that students with ASC can experience in a crowded classroom, you should make sure that they do not become too dependent on technology and isolated from their peers. Make sure they still participate in some group activities, and that technology is enhancing their school experience and learning.

Using the internet

Making learning English meaningful and relevant

Some learners with SEN find abstract concepts and theories difficult to grasp. Allowing them to use the internet to look up information in class makes learning meaningful and relevant. They can focus on actual events in real time and find solutions to real-life problems. Students acquire key information instantly and receive answers to questions as they arise in class. They also come to realize how useful English skills are when surfing the internet.

The growth of AT has given students with SEN opportunities to overcome barriers to learning and express themselves in new and exciting ways. There are many tools and resources for teachers which are free and simple to use, making the task of including and inspiring all of our students so much easier.

Part 3

Types of SEN: information and practical teaching strategies

7

Dyslexia

I hate English lessons. The teacher says I'm lazy, but I'm trying really hard.
I just hate reading aloud, and copying from the board takes ages.
ELENA, AGED 9

Students such as Elena can be frustrating to teach. They appear to have good potential but seem lazy in class. They can often express themselves fluently when they speak, but seem slow and disengaged when they have to read or write. These students may have dyslexia. This chapter will look at ways to understand what it's like to have dyslexia, ways of spotting it in class, and teaching strategies which can help.

What is dyslexia?

Dyslexia is an information processing difficulty which primarily affects reading, spelling, and writing. Learners will typically have problems with phonological processing (linking sounds to words), visual processing (seeing words and letters), and working memory (remembering what has just been said). They may also have problems with organization, sequencing, and number skills.

Indicators

Signs that a student in your class might have dyslexia include:
- poor written work compared with speaking ability
- slow and hesitant reading and misreading of words
- difficulty matching a sound to a letter
- seeing and writing letters as flipped or reversed ('b' mistaken for 'd' or 'p'; 'n' for 'c' or 'u')
- seeing letters move around or becoming blurred on the page
- quickly forgetting what they have read or have just been told
- being slow to process language
- problems with organization and being on time
- daydreaming and not paying attention in class
- complaints of feeling tired when reading or writing.

Ask yourself

Does this remind you of any of your students? How have you responded to them in class?

Diagnosis

Be careful not to assume that a student who is showing one or two of the signs must be dyslexic. Reversing letters, for example, is very common when students are learning to write in a new script, and younger children often tire easily in language lessons. However, if a student is showing several of the signs listed above, it could be useful to ask for an assessment from an educational psychologist.

Self-esteem

Many students with dyslexia lose confidence and suffer from low self-esteem at school because they find learning in class slow and difficult. They may think of themselves as stupid. They can lose their motivation to learn, and fall behind their peers. When this happens some students misbehave to avoid showing the teacher that they can't do the work.

The teacher has a vital role to play in encouraging and supporting these students when they are losing confidence. They are often making more effort than other students when reading and writing, even if this doesn't show in their work. So be careful not to label students as lazy. By reacting in the wrong way to students' problems, teachers may make things worse. Here are some students' comments on their negative experiences:

I thought I was stupid. I couldn't keep up and the teacher didn't care.

I ask teachers to explain … so they explain again using the same words, I don't understand, and they get angry.

It's important to be clear with students that dyslexia doesn't mean people can't succeed – at school or in life. Dyslexia is not linked to low intelligence. Many people with dyslexia have great strengths – they can be effective verbal communicators, visually talented, or more able to think creatively than others.

Try this ☞　**Famous people**

Ask students if they know of any famous people with dyslexia, and if not, to find out on the internet. Ask students to list the contributions these people have made to the world.

Building confidence

There are many things a teacher can do to help students build their confidence with learning. Explain that we need to practise and make mistakes in order to get better at anything – for example, learning how to ride a bicycle. This is needed in language learning too.

Try this ☞　**Share mistakes**

Take the most common mistakes that the class made on a test and go through them together. The more open everyone is about their mistakes, the less important they may seem.

Encourage students to think about what it takes to make them feel positive and confident. Use the imaginary wristband activity (see page 30) to illustrate this. Many students with dyslexia feel anxious as soon as they look at a page of text, or the teacher asks them to write. If they can feel positive before they begin these tasks, they're more likely to work well.

Try this ☞   **Mood music**

Choose music to play in your lessons which improves the mood of your students. Experiment with different types and involve your class in choosing the best music for decreasing anxiety and promoting learning. Students can even imagine the music in their heads before attempting tests.

Find different ways for students to demonstrate what they know in class. Students with dyslexia will lose confidence if they always have to write down their answers in their books or on worksheets.

Try this ☞   **Recording**

Use audio devices and, if your school allows it, encourage students to record their answers with their smartphones or MP4 players. Students with dyslexia will find it easier to say the answer than to write it.

Try this ☞   **Chat show**

Use drama activities to help students express their thoughts and show their creativity. Ask groups of students to perform a talk show where the presenter interviews the group about what they have learned.

 *Getting it right*

Positive feedback

Make sure that feedback to students on their progress is encouraging and focuses on any improvements made. Be careful not to label their slow progress as laziness or as lack of effort. Give praise and encouragement as often as possible, particularly focusing on skills other than literacy.

Dyslexia – problem or gift?

Dyslexia can be seen as a strength. Check students are able to describe their strengths by encouraging them to think about what they're good at.

People with dyslexia can often:
- see the big picture – or hold an overall view of how something works
- be intuitive and able to make new connections between things and ideas
- think in 3D and have a good sense of spatial reasoning
- succeed as entrepreneurs or in work that involves complex problem-solving or creativity.

Try this ☞   **The inventor**

Ask students to think of new uses for everyday objects. For example, *A pen can be a...* Groups of students think of as many different ways as possible to use a pen in a different way.

Try this ☞   **President for the day**

Use activities which require 'big-picture' thinking. For example, *If I were president for the day, what would I change?* Students with dyslexia are often better at this type of activity compared to others which involve a lot of detail.

Practical teaching strategies

Students with dyslexia have specific problems with the processing of sounds and words. In particular, they can't always hear the difference between sounds, and often find it difficult to match the sounds of English to the written word.

Multisensory teaching

Multisensory teaching will help students with dyslexia. Using multiple senses (so students see, hear, feel, and do it) reinforces their learning. Words and letters can be traced in different ways – for example, in the air, in sand, on a partner's back, or made in 3D using clay.

Try this ☞ Chair verbs

Make grammar physical. Put five chairs in a line and ask five students to sit on them. Each chair represents a personal pronoun – *I, you, he* or *she, we,* and *they*. Choose a verb and ask each student to conjugate the verb for their pronoun, for example: *I play, you play, he or she plays, we play, they play*. Students then rotate seats and do it again with another verb.

Try this ☞ My words

Students work in pairs and choose words they want to practise spelling. They take it in turns to trace their words on their partner's back. Their partner tries to guess what the word is.

Try this ☞ Making words from bodies

Students work in teams of four or five. They choose a four- or five-letter word. Each student makes one letter in the word using their body. They show the word to the other groups, who must guess the word. This is a fun activity which can also act as an energizer in class.

Help with visual processing

Students with dyslexia don't have an **internal sight lexicon**. This means they find it difficult to remember how letters and words look in their mind and memorize how sounds link to letter symbols. When they try to spell a word, they often try to say the letters aloud or in their head, but can't remember the order of the letters. This auditory way of spelling words is usually unsuccessful. Teachers need to help students develop strategies to visualize the words in their minds and remember them.

Try this ☞ Word box

Students keep their own word box of high-frequency words which they use to review vocabulary and test themselves.

Try this ☞ **Magic spelling**

Hold up the target word written on a piece of card. Ask students to look at the word, then close their eyes and imagine the word in their mind. Tell them to open their eyes again and check their image of the word with the real word. Do this a few times. Ask students to tell you the letters they can see in their mind. Encourage students to hold the word as a photo in their mind.

Try this ☞ **Velcro words**

Put a word bank of high-frequency words on the wall, using Velcro strips for each word. Students borrow words from the wall when they need a reminder of how to spell them. Students can create their own word banks and keep them in a book, on their mobile phone, or on a bookmark or key ring.

Try this ☞ **Colour-coding**

Use different colours to highlight the patterns of words and to break down the sounds into manageable chunks. For example: *boat, coat, moat*.

Help with working memory

Teachers often don't realize that one key indicator of dyslexia is poor working memory – a memory system which stores and works with information needed for everyday activities (see page 24). Strategies you can use to improve their working memory include breaking learning down into small steps, using clear, multisensory instructions, checklists, visual aids, and colour-coding of work.

Games

Games are a fun way to help students develop their working memory. Students with dyslexia may find these games difficult but should be encouraged to take part.

Try this ☞ **Change things**

In pairs, ask students to look at their partners and to remember everything about their appearance. Tell one student in each pair to go outside and to change three things about their appearance; for example, to put their watch on the other wrist. Then their partner must identify the three differences.

Try this ☞ **Odd one out**

Give students four pictures or words of vocabulary items which they know. Ask them to say which picture is the odd one out. For example: *chair, desk, bed, whiteboard*.

Visual processing

Students with visual processing problems find it difficult to track the words on the page when reading. They begin reading the start of the sentence and their eyes jump to the end of another sentence. You can check whether you suffer from visual stress at www.visualstresstest.com.

Try this ☞ **Self-tracking**

Tell students to stop at regular intervals and ask themselves: *What have I just read? What are the key words?* Ask students to underline the key words.

Try this ☞ **Line tracking**

Use something physical to help track words on a line. You can use a ruler or make a ruler with a section cut out which frames the text you want to read and covers up the rest.

This would mean that the part of the text I'm reading is within the cut out lines and the ruler covers up the part I'm not reading.

There are also computer programs and apps for tracking text (see page 47).

Try this ☞ **Background colour**

Some students will read more easily from certain colours of paper or certain types of colour transparencies (see page 46), so try making photocopies on off-white paper (salmon-pink, grey, or beige).

Support with written tasks

Students with dyslexia may find writing tiring and difficult. They will need support and encouragement. It helps if you provide photocopied notes, printouts, writing templates, and lists of spellings and key phrases. Ensure that your board writing is well spaced out if the student needs to read or copy it. There are also many computer programs and apps which can help students with writing (see Chapter 6 for ideas).

Try this ☞ **Mind maps**

Get students to draw mind maps to record important information. Students with dyslexia can often visualize the whole page of a mind map, but struggle to remember a list of words.

Try this ☞ **Rehearsal**

Encourage students to think about what they want to write before they start. They could tell you their ideas, put them in a mind map, or record them on a mobile device.

Ask yourself

What would your mind map for what you have learned about dyslexia look like? (See Appendix 3, page 101.) What do you think are the advantages of mind mapping?

8   Dyspraxia

Gio is really disorganized. He's always late for class, and when he does eventually arrive he's noisy and disruptive, dropping things out of his bag and bumping into other desks on his way to his seat.

ALICIA, SECONDARY TEACHER, ITALY

Do you have a student like Gio? He might be clumsy and disorganized because he has dyspraxia.

What is dyspraxia?

Dyspraxia is a **developmental coordination difficulty**, which means difficulty coordinating the body and muscles to perform the actions needed to carry out tasks. Students have problems with **gross motor skills** such as running and jumping, as well as **fine motor skills** such as picking something up with their fingers. At home, getting dressed or using cutlery can be problematic, and in class, using a pencil can be very difficult for them. Students can also have problems with organizing their work and following instructions, as well as with short-term memory, speaking and listening, social skills, and friendships.

Strengths

Students with dyspraxia will often find creative ways to remember and learn skills and information. They can show great perseverance and tenacity in their learning, and these are qualities which you should recognize and value. As with all students with SEN, it's important to build on students' strengths and interests.

Indicators

The main indicators for dyspraxia are:
- difficulty with balance and coordination (problems with everyday skills such as tying shoelaces and getting dressed)
- poor writing, drawing, and copying skills
- limited concentration and poor listening skills
- difficulty remembering more than one or two instructions at once
- understanding and using language very literally
- difficulty with social skills (for example, forming friendships)
- becoming emotional and easily upset or excited (sometimes accompanied by motor activity such as hand flapping or clapping)
- difficulty sleeping, including suffering from nightmares, and a tendency to have headaches, including migraines.

 **Getting it right**

Students as individuals

Remember to treat all students as individuals. Most students with dyspraxia won't have all of these difficulties, but their problems will vary in severity, from mild to severe. Don't label students as lazy or disorganized, because this kind of judgement impacts negatively on their learning and self-esteem. Try to find out as much as possible about your students and their barriers to learning.

Practical teaching strategies

Writing

Difficulties with fine motor skills mean that students with dyspraxia often have trouble with writing. This becomes more obvious as they get older, and can have a negative impact on learning and assessment, as the teacher may not be able to read their written work. It's therefore important to model good writing. Show students how to hold the pen correctly in a tripod grip and write clearly on the board. Use different coloured pens for each line so that students can easily keep track of what you write. Use worksheets and handouts so students don't have to do a lot of copying from the board.

Try to understand the particular problem students have with writing. If they're gripping their pen tightly and pressing down very hard on the page, suggest they take regular breaks to relax. If they have strange posture, check they're sitting in an upright position with both feet resting on the floor. Provide a sloping desk, or if this isn't possible, encourage students to place their arm on an angled folder or book. It usually helps if students place their writing paper to the side and not in the middle of the desk. It is also worth bearing in mind that most students write better on lined paper.

Try this ☞ **Starting dots**

Encourage students to put a dot at the beginning of each line in their exercise book before they begin any written work. This helps them to see and remember where each line starts.

Try this ☞ **Paper clips**

Allow students to use Blu-tack or paper clips to hold their paper down and secure the page they're writing on.

Try this ☞ **My left hand**

Teach students the English directions 'left' and 'right'. Show them how you can make the letter 'L' with your left hand by holding it up in front of you, with the forefinger pointing up and the thumb horizontal. This will help students remember that 'left' begins with L, as well as reminding them which side is left.

Try this ☞ **Writing in the air**

When students are learning to write new words, let them practise writing the word in front of them in the air with their finger. This will help them 'feel' the shape of the word.

✓ *Getting it right*   **Choice of pen**

Don't insist that students use a certain type of pen or pencil for writing. Allow them to use pens they're comfortable with: felt-tip pens, biros, or pencils. Encourage them to experiment with chunky pens/pencils and ones with a grip.

It's important to be aware of how difficult a task involving motor skills will be for students with dyspraxia. Coursebook activities such as 'Describe and draw' or 'Listen and draw' can be too challenging. Dictations can also cause problems, because students have problems writing quickly enough to do traditional dictations. Encourage them to learn to touch-type, and allow them, if possible, to type their work on the computer. Voice recognition software can be a helpful tool for these students because they find the action of writing very tiring. They can use it to convert spoken words into text (see page 45).

Try this ☞ **Drawing activities**

Differentiate the task by giving students a partially filled-in outline of the drawing, or by allowing them to give the instructions for drawing instead of doing the drawing themselves.

Try this ☞ **Dictogloss**

Read out the text (or sentences, for younger students) and tell students to listen but not write anything down. Read it again and give them a chance to write down any words they remember. Then ask them in pairs to try and reconstruct the text. Pairs can then join up to form groups of four and help each other. Students can contribute their ideas verbally. Compare the texts at the end.

Speech and Language

Students with dyspraxia may have speech and language difficulties in their L1. It can cause problems with their receptive language and productive speech.

Receptive

Students will often need support in processing language, such as understanding and following instructions. Help them by giving instructions in written and visual forms as well as spoken. Break tasks down into small components and chunks. Sit students with partners who can help explain tasks.

Try this ☞ **Lesson outlines**

Show the different stages of a lesson on the side of the board by representing them visually using symbols, such as an ear for a listening activity and a speech bubble for speaking practice. Remove the symbols from the board as you complete each stage.

Productive

Students will often find speaking in class embarrassing and difficult. They need more time to say what they want. Give them this time to formulate responses, and allow them to answer questions in non-verbal ways. If necessary, seat students near you so they can ask for help more easily.

Try this ☞ **Visual prompts**

Teach students how to ask you to repeat something by using a signal, for example, a card they can turn over on their desk or hold up and show you.

Forming words

Dyspraxia can also cause physical difficulties with the movement of the mouth and tongue. Students may struggle to form words and be difficult to understand. They can have problems choosing the right words to answer questions. If students are already having these problems in their L1, they may have similar problems in learning English. However, by showing students with dyspraxia how sounds are made, the English class can provide an opportunity for them to learn English pronunciation at the same pace as their peers..

Try this ☞ **Phoneme hoot**

Make a set of cards, each with a sound you want to practise on it. You can use the phonemic symbols or words with the key sound underlined, for example: *sheep*. Students walk around saying their sound but not showing their word, looking for a partner with the same sound. Encourage them to exaggerate their mouth and lip movements.

Try this ☞ **Picture my mouth**

Show students how sounds are made in the mouth by physical demonstration and pictures. Focus on the use of the tongue and the shape of the mouth. Exaggerate the movements in a fun way. Most students will have difficulties with pronunciation in a new language, and all of them will benefit from this practice.

Try this ☞ **Silent dictation**

When teaching minimal pairs of contrasting sounds, such as ship/sheep, show students how the mouth and tongue work with each sound. Then dictate some simple words, mouthing the word without sound. Ask students in pairs to identify which word you're saying. Let students practise the same activity in pairs.

Organization

Students with dyspraxia have difficulties with working memory and organization. They find it difficult to remember schoolbooks and school timetables. They often arrive in the wrong place at the wrong time with the wrong books! This can be frustrating for teachers, but you can help them in simple ways – for example, by making sure your classroom is well organized and clearly labelled so students know where to find things. Try to be patient with students. Offer them spare books and pens when they need them or loose leaf folders they can put their work in. Work with parents/carers to set up support strategies at home. They can check with their child in the morning about books and equipment needed for the day.

Try this ☞ **Lists**

Get students to use Post-it notes or lists stuck next to the door at home and school to use as reminders.

Try this ☞ **Visual timetables**

Get students to write the things that they do each day at school on strips of card. Encourage them to add a picture to illustrate different activities – this will help them remember, for example, that they need their library books on Monday and their sports kit on Friday. If possible, allow students to laminate the strips of card. (See Appendix 2, page 100.)

Try this ☞ **Colour-coding work materials**

Teach or revise the English words for colours and school subjects and then ask students to associate a different colour with each subject, for example, blue for English. Encourage students to colour-code different subject books to help them remember which ones to bring to each lesson.

Sequencing

Students are likely to have problems with language activities that involve sequencing and putting things in order. They get confused about what order to do activities in and where to begin. They need activities which practise these skills.

Try this ☞ **Line-ups**

Use line-ups to practise a variety of language points. Students can line up in the order of their birthday months, or according to the time of day they got up, or the number of brothers and sisters they have. Older students can line up according to how much they like or know about something.

✓ *Getting it right* **Self-help skills**

Share strategies with students on how to remember things, because then they will start to develop the skills they need to help themselves. Be sure to praise them when they get things right – and try not to criticize when they get things wrong. You and your students will feel better for focusing on the positive rather than the negative.

Social difficulties

As a result of their speech and language difficulties and their general clumsiness, students with dyspraxia often have immature social skills and find it difficult to make friends. The teacher needs to help them join in with their classmates when engaging in group work and games. Try to include activities which promote cooperation, and at the same time work with students to prevent them getting over-excited in class.

Try this ☞ **Matching pictures**

When you want students to work in random pairs, give out pictures which have been cut into two. Students search for the person who has the other half of their picture. You can do this with beginnings and endings of sentences, or words with similar sounds or meanings.

Try this ☞ **Noise barometer**

Make a noise barometer with a sliding arrow. The top of the barometer is 'Too noisy' and the bottom is 'Just right'. Move the arrow up and down according to class noise levels. This helps students with dyspraxia become aware of when they are getting too loud and excited.

Confidence and self-esteem

The combination of learning and social difficulties can cause students with dyspraxia to suffer from low confidence and poor self-esteem. They will benefit in particular from a peer support or a 'buddy' system to help them develop friendships with other students. Ask students if they would like to explain to the class what it feels like to have dyspraxia (see page 15) because this can sometimes be helpful. Remember to reward students for their non-academic skills, particularly perseverance (see page 30). Be aware that sometimes students will complain about headaches as a way of avoiding having to do something new and possibly demoralizing.

Try this ☞ **Walk in my shoes**

Bring in a pair of thick gloves, a piece of string, and some beads. Ask student volunteers to put on the gloves and to pick up the beads, one by one, and thread them onto the piece of string. Students will probably find this very difficult and frustrating. Explain to the class that this is what it feels like to have dyspraxia. Alternatively, ask students to cut out a shape from some thick card with a small pair of scissors.

 *Getting it right*

Motor skills

Think about the level of motor skills needed for some of your activities. If your lesson involves making things and cutting things up, get students to work in pairs and allow the student with dyspraxia to read the instructions for their partner to follow. If an activity involves running or catching, be aware that students with dyspraxia might not enjoy the activity and could get upset. You could ask them to help you monitor the activity instead.

9 Attention deficit hyperactivity disorder (ADHD)

> Jozef is like a spinning top. He's always calling out, whirling around the classroom, not finishing activities, interrupting other students, and taking their things. I get a headache and he really annoys other students.
>
> MARKUS, SECONDARY TEACHER, GERMANY

Do you have students like Jozef? They may have attention deficit hyperactivity disorder or ADHD. It can be difficult to manage these students. Their behaviour can stop them from learning and can interrupt the learning of other students. In this chapter we will consider ways of understanding ADHD, the needs and challenges of students with ADHD, and teaching strategies to support them in class.

What is ADHD?

Traditionally ADHD has been known as 'attention deficit hyperactivity disorder'. But there is a preference nowadays to call it a 'difference', not a 'disorder'. 'Disorder' suggests there is something wrong with the person, while 'difference' suggests they simply have a different way of thinking and behaving. Your thinking on this subject will probably influence how you teach students with ADHD.

Ask yourself

Does it matter whether we use the word 'disorder' or 'difference'? Which term do you think is a better description of students with ADHD? Why?

Indicators

The main indicators for ADHD are:
- hyperactivity (or difficulty in staying still and keeping focus)
- inattention (or difficulty in sustaining attention)
- impulsivity (or difficulty in controlling impulses).

Hyperactivity

Students may:
- fidget and move around constantly in their seat
- leave their seat without permission
- be restless and seek physical activity, such as running and climbing
- talk non-stop and find it hard to be quiet even when asked.

Inattention

Students may:
- make careless mistakes in their work and in other activities
- be easily distracted from tasks and play activities
- not seem to listen when the teacher is speaking directly to them
- not follow instructions and not finish work
- have difficulty organizing activities
- be forgetful
- often lose things
- avoid tasks that require focus and concentration – for example, homework.

Impulsivity

Students may:
- have difficulty waiting their turn in class and in games
- interrupt conversations
- shout out answers before a question has been completed.

Diagnosis

A clinical diagnosis of ADHD is usually only made if a student shows six or more of the behaviours from the Inattention list or six or more from the combined Hyperactivity and Impulsivity lists, with these behaviours occurring at home and at school.

 *Getting it right*

Help not diagnosis

If you have a student with these behaviours, don't automatically assume they have ADHD. Students might have problems paying attention in class for many reasons, such as being hungry or tired, or finding the work too easy or difficult. Talk to other teachers and the parents/carers. Describe what you've noticed in class and ask if this behaviour happens at home. Then discuss a way forward together. Don't suggest a diagnosis of ADHD yourself.

What causes ADHD?

There are no clear causes of ADHD. Some research suggests it might be genetic and some people believe diet plays a factor. However, ADHD is an emotive topic and there is ongoing debate between experts about its causes and treatment, particularly about the benefits of medication and/or behavioural modification programs. Whatever you believe, you need to understand the ways that ADHD affects learning in class.

Research by neuroscientists suggests that students with ADHD have deficits in their executive functioning and working memory. Executive functioning (EF) is a term psychologists use to describe the tasks our brains perform that are necessary for thinking, acting, and solving problems. Poor EF negatively affects learning. Our internal voice is also part of our EF. Our internal voice is the private voice we use for talking to ourselves, allowing us to reflect on our behaviour and to regulate our actions.

Ask yourself

What would it be like not to have an internal voice? How do you think this might affect the way you behave?

Strengths

Students with ADHD are often emotionally honest, energetic, and creative. It can be annoying when they shout out loudly that the lesson is boring, but they can be very positive when they are enjoying an activity. Use their natural energy and creativity in activities involving drama and writing. For example, ask students to change the endings of stories, or ask them to rewrite stories with deliberate mistakes for other students to correct.

Try this ☞　**Through different eyes**

Ask students to retell a story through the eyes of another character or even an object in the story. For example, in a story where a car hits a lamppost, students can tell the story from the view of the lamppost. In a description of a room with a teddy bear in it, students can describe what the teddy bear sees.

Try this ☞　**Senses stories**

Ask students to rewrite or retell a familiar story with a focus on one of the senses. For example, they should focus on all the sights, all the sounds, all the feelings, all the tastes, or all the smells in the story. Younger learners can draw what they would see or feel and make the sounds they would hear.

Classroom management

Class dynamics

The way students with ADHD behave in class can have a negative effect on the other students. They find it difficult to work with them in groups because they don't wait their turn, interrupt conversations, make silly remarks, and are easily distracted. Although some students find this behaviour funny, most are irritated by it and students with ADHD can become socially isolated.

Try this ☞　**Self-talk**

Help students to practise self-talk about positive classroom behaviour so that they understand what they should do, for example:
I should sit in my seat during lesson time.
I should let my partner finish speaking before I start talking.

Try this ☞　**Thoughts box**

Tell students to keep a small box on their desk in which they can place any thoughts or questions they want to ask the teacher but which can wait for an answer. This should encourage them to stop shouting out. Set aside time at the end of the lesson to collect the questions.

Students with ADHD often lie about events and make up improbable stories – perhaps to create entertainment for themselves because they are bored. They often stick by their stories even in the face of disapproval because they seem to believe in them, causing teachers and other students to become confused and/or angry.

Try this ☞ **Spot the lie**

Turn lying into a creative task. Ask students to rewrite a comprehension passage, changing it to include at least three lies. Younger students can simply change three words. For example, *John likes ice cream* can become *John doesn't like ice cream*. Other students have to spot the lies.

Classroom environment

Students with ADHD need a calm, orderly classroom. Keep your classroom as tidy as possible. Organize wall displays with clear focal points and keep them uncluttered. Untidy material on the wall will distract students with ADHD. Seat students near you and always away from distractions, such as window blinds and radiators. Some students benefit from having their own desk. They can be anxious about holding the teacher's attention and will try to keep the teacher continually by their side.

✓ *Getting it right*

Help with anxiety

Help students with their anxiety by setting clear time limits for work and letting them know when you will be back to help. If you couldn't come back by the agreed time, acknowledge their concerns by saying: *Maybe you thought I had forgotten you, but I hadn't.*

Classroom rules and rewards

Establish a few clear, positively phrased classroom rules, with reminders, rewards, and sanctions. Always notice and praise appropriate behaviour immediately by saying, for example: *Thank you for waiting with your hand up*. If you have to discipline a student, say what you want to happen and repeat it in a firm calm voice – avoid constantly rephrasing and explaining. Students with ADHD have short attention spans and live in the present, and once something has happened they soon forget about it. This means that rewards and sanctions only work in short timeframes.

Try this ☞ **Motivating rewards**

Let students choose their own reward for good work or behaviour. Some students are motivated by goal charts or stickers, some by having a job such as looking after the class pet, some by longer computer time, and some by being given a positive note to take home.

Try this ☞ **Energy burst**

When the student is becoming hyperactive in class, have an agreed 'timeout' plan, which allows the student to go to a designated area and do something physical to use up energy – for example, jogging on the spot.

Managing feelings

Students with ADHD can become isolated, withdrawn, and lacking in confidence. It's vital to remain positive in the way you deal with them and to give them opportunities to express how they're feeling in an appropriate way. This doesn't mean you have to fix how they're feeling – you just need to give them a chance to talk about it. Showing confidence in students by giving them class responsibilities can also be useful.

Try this ☞   **Rate my feeling**

 ———————————————— Marcos
                                        ✗

Draw a line on the board with a frowning face at one end and a smiling face at the other. Students come up to the board and write their name at a point on the line for how they're feeling at that moment. Or students can rate on a scale of 1–10 how they're feeling by holding up their fingers (10 = feeling great, 1 = feeling terrible).

Try this ☞   **Safety inspectors**

Give students with ADHD jobs to teach them about safe behaviour. For example, they can be safety inspectors with a safety checklist for equipment (computer cables, etc.). Younger students can focus on keeping the classroom and desks tidy.

Managing inattention

Students with ADHD need help and support to pay attention in class. When you want to attract their attention, be sure to make eye contact with them, say their name, and check that they are looking at you before you start speaking. You should also give clear time limits for completing work, and warnings when time is nearly up.

Try this ☞   **Count down**

Give students a warning that time is nearly up by counting down showing the numbers on your fingers and saying: *5, 4, 3, 2, 1 … stop!*

Students with ADHD often have trouble staying focused on longer pieces of work. They forget what to do, and get distracted or bored with the task. The presentation of their work can therefore be untidy because they aren't paying attention to their writing. Other students might seem to be inattentive because they're preoccupied or worried about something. Explain that it's normal for people's minds to wander and it's impossible to pay attention if your mind is full up with anxious thoughts. Tell them that the trick is to notice that we have become distracted and to know how to bring our mind back to our work.

Long homework tasks can also be problematic. Help students by thinking of ways to make it fun, relevant, and not too time-consuming.

Try this ☞ **English in my life**

Ask students to find English words on the packaging of food products at home, listen to a song in English, teach their parents/carers the words of the day, or find five things on the way home that they know in English.

Try this ☞ **Short computer activities**

Working on computer programs such as Wordshark (see page 46) allows students to do short quick activities with instant responses. Using headphones can help block out distractions.

Try this ☞ **Graph paper**

Get students to write on graph paper instead of lined paper. The grid patterns seem to hold their interest more effectively than lined paper.

Try this ☞ **My hero**

Ask students to invent a 'superhero of the brain' – an imaginary helper who can bring their attention back when it wanders. Students can draw their own hero and keep her/him in their books as a reminder.

Try this ☞ **Mindful breathing**

Take a brain break with students and ask them to practise **mindful breathing** to improve their focus. Breathe in through the nose for a count of four and out through the mouth for a count of four. Do this a few times.

Try this ☞ **Worry box**

Make a worry box or use a large envelope for students to write down any private worries they want the teacher to know. Put this on or near your desk. Take time to empty it, and deal with any issues privately if necessary.

Managing impulsivity

Students with ADHD are often very impulsive and need help with self-regulation. They tend to want to talk a lot – including both asking and answering questions – but they don't usually want to listen. It's important to plan activities and develop routines that train them and other students to listen to each other.

Try this ☞ **Lolly sticks**

Use different ways of selecting students to answer questions. One way is to keep lolly sticks with students' names written on them in a cup on your desk. When you ask the class a question, get a student to pick out a stick. The student whose name is on the stick should answer your question.

Try this ☞ **Brain, book, buddy, boss**

When students aren't sure about how to do something, encourage them to use the four Bs for independent work:

1   Think again (Brain)
2   Look in your book (Book)
3   Ask a friend (Buddy)
4   Ask the boss (the teacher!) (Boss)

Try this ☞ **Information-gap activities**

Use information-gap activities where students are given different information and have to share it with a partner.

Managing hyperactivity

Students with ADHD find it difficult to sit still for any length of time. They need opportunities to let off energy – both verbally and physically – and you can build these into your lessons. For example, while you're talking or giving instructions to the class, allow students to:

• stand up at the back of the room
• doodle and draw while you're talking
• underline texts in different colours
• use a small stress ball to fiddle with.

Try this ☞ **30/60 seconds grab**

Ask students to choose a letter and to think of nouns beginning with this letter. Students work in pairs. Give each pair a coin. In pairs, one student uses one of the nouns as a topic, holds the coin in their outstretched palm, and talks for 60 seconds non-stop on that topic. As they're talking, their partner tries to grab the coin. Lower-level learners can choose vocabulary areas to name as many words as possible from that area in 30 seconds.

10

Social, emotional, and behavioural difficulties (SEBD)

Mrs Bergman is always shouting at me. I don't care. I hate English anyway – I can't do it. I just want to have a laugh with my friends.

ANDREAS, AGED 12

Students like Andreas can be very difficult to teach. Their behaviour and attitude annoy and frustrate their teachers. They might be showing that they have social, emotional, and behavioural difficulties.

What are SEBD?

It can sometimes be difficult to decide when poor behaviour should be treated as a special educational need. A certain amount of subjective judgment is involved in recognizing that students have SEBD, and teachers have different levels of tolerance for types of behaviour. As a language teacher, you might be happy to accept loud talking, walking around, and laughing, whereas a science teacher might find it unacceptable or even dangerous. Student behaviour can also change according to the time of day, their mood, and what they're studying.

In order to get a clear picture of a student's needs, it is important to observe and record their behaviour in all classes and with a variety of teachers. Students can only be considered to have SEBD if they have problems across a range of subjects, with different teachers, and at different times of day.

Indicators

Students with SEBD can:
- find it difficult to form and maintain friendships with peers and teachers
- experience extreme mood swings – very happy one minute and unhappy the next
- become physically or verbally aggressive to staff or other students and react negatively to changes to their routine or to teaching staff
- behave in a way which is unsafe and likely to injure themselves and others – for example, swinging on doors or standing on tables
- do things to attract attention – for example, shouting loudly, making silly noises
- refuse to follow instructions, for example, not leaving the room when asked, or not doing their work or homework
- react inappropriately to correction or praise – for example, tearing up work when it's praised or shouting when corrected by the teacher

- have a limited concentration span and spend little time on-task, sometimes becoming aggressive or withdrawn when under pressure, or losing their temper with their work.

Ask yourself

Do you think that SEBD is really a special educational need? Do you think these students need extra help or just extra discipline?

 **Getting it right**

Extra provision

It's important to understand that students with certain types of extreme behaviour are not coping in class and are not learning. If normal classroom management isn't working with such students, this means they have special educational needs. As such, it is necessary to consider what extra provision can be put into place to support them.

Does punishment work?

Sometimes the school's first reaction with these students is to apply stronger discipline and more severe punishments. This doesn't usually work if it is the only strategy used. It's understandable to think that students simply need to be better controlled, but students with SEBD are more vulnerable and troubled than they appear. Their own behaviour often frightens them and they want adults to understand and help them.

 **Getting it right**

Behaviour as communication

See behaviour as a communication of students' needs and think about what it means. Try to empathize with students and understand their behaviour, because your attitude and those of other adults will have the greatest impact on them. Remember you can't control anything except your own reaction, so keep calm and manage your own emotions.

Strengths

Students with SEBD are usually very honest in their responses and feelings and will appreciate honesty and support from the teacher. This means that when you do develop a relationship with them, they recognize the effort you have made. Students with SEBD often have strong opinions and leadership skills, which you can develop in class by involving them in making decisions and carrying out certain jobs.

Show that you have high expectations for them, even when they're misbehaving. For example, say: *It's great you want to join in the discussion. I just need you to remember to wait your turn*. Mention any strengths you know they have and link this with expected behaviour. For example: *I know you're funny, but you can be funny without being unkind to others*.

 **Getting it right**

Responsibility

Give students a job as a normal part of your classroom routine, not as a reward. Students with SEBD find it difficult to work towards a reward and rarely achieve the target. It's easier for them to behave well in order to keep the job than to gain it.

Causes

Environment

Students with SEBD may have learned patterns of behaviour and thinking in reaction to the environments they have been living in, which may be uncertain, inconsistent, and sometimes dangerous. Perhaps they have not had experience of adults who can care for them in a safe way, or have had experience of adults who weren't able to cope for other reasons.

If children do not receive consistent, sensitive care, they learn not to trust adults. They also develop high levels of cortisol (the main stress hormone) in their bodies. High stress levels during early brain development can cause too many neural connections to be made in the parts responsible for anxiety and impulsive responses – and too few connections in the parts responsible for empathy, logic, planning, and reasoning. As such, the stress response in these children becomes too sensitive, causing their brains to behave as if they are under constant attack and the **reptilian brain** (the oldest part of the brain) to be overused.

This means students with SEBD often have brains programmed to expect attack at all times, and will very quickly resort to a **fight or flight** response. Rational thinking is impossible when the brain is in this mode.

Fight or flight behaviour may show up in class when:
- work seems too difficult
- the teacher corrects the student
- routines are changed without warning.

 **Getting it right**

Left-brain tasks

When students are in a state of fight and flight, calm them down by giving them logical, **left-brain** tasks such as sorting, categorizing, putting things in order, or tidying up. Don't try to talk to them about how they feel or why they behaved badly. Their brain needs to calm down first with logical, no-risk activities.

Hypervigilance

Some children learn that they need to pay attention to every mood and action of adults. In class these students are unable to focus on one task or activity for long, because they are constantly checking the safety of their environment and the mood of the people in it. We call this behaviour 'hypervigilance'.

Students who have had poor experiences of adult care in their early years find it difficult to trust teachers. Some are so preoccupied and anxious about life outside the classroom, or perceived threats in the classroom, that their brains are overloaded. You need to help these students trust you and feel safe so that they are able to learn.

Try this ☞ **Reptilian brains**

Teach students about the reptilian brain and how we needed it in prehistoric times to recognize danger. With younger children you can use a toy dinosaur or reptile. Older students can draw a cartoon representation. Bring out the toy or cartoon when students are angry or upset as a gentle reminder to calm down and refocus.

Try this    **Frame it**

> Frame worksheet activities to make the page feel safe.
> For example, put vocabulary in a word snake, or put a picture frame around grammar exercises.

Learning through play

In successful classroom learning, students are happy to share the teacher's attention, can take turns in speaking, and can cope with making mistakes. Most people learn these skills in play as a child. Some students with SEBD didn't have enough opportunities to play and therefore didn't acquire these important skills for learning. So you might, for example, be teaching a fourteen-year-old who has the play skills of a two-year-old.

Try this    **Pelmanism**

Create pairs of cards where one card has a picture of a vocabulary item, and the other card has the written word. Students place the cards face down on the table and take turns at trying to find a matching pair by turning over two cards at a time. If players find a match, they keep it and have another go. If they don't, they turn the cards face down again. Older students can practise **homophones** or **homonyms**, or match verbs with their tense forms.

✔ *Getting it right*   **Games**

Use games to practise skills such as turn-taking and losing. Don't give up if students break the rules or act in a silly manner – this is a learning opportunity. Pause the game and check the rules. Check that everyone knows why we need rules (to make it fun and safe). Acknowledge difficulties by saying, *It's hard to lose, no one likes it, but let's try again.*

Classroom management

Positive language

Let students know what you want them to do, rather than what you don't want them to do. Use the language of 'need' rather than obligation. For example, say: *I need you to sit here now.*

Give students a positive reason for your classroom decisions. For example, if you want them to sit near you, say: *I'd like to be able to hear your opinions and check you're doing your best work.*

Link rules to learning and safety. For example, say: *We agreed on these rules so that we can all learn as much as possible and feel safe doing it.*

If students break a rule, use it as a learning opportunity. Draw parallels to rules in other areas of their life to help students self-regulate their emotions and behaviour. For example, say: *How do you remember the rules in football? How do you stop yourself getting angry with the referee? Can you do that in class?*

If students go off-task, don't focus on this in case it causes an unnecessary power struggle. Redirect their attention to the activity in hand. For example, say: *That first paragraph has some great ideas. How are you going to develop them in the next part?*

Developing trust

Students with SEBD need to learn to trust the teacher in order to learn, because those who misbehave often only get noticed by the teacher when they do something wrong. Remember to notice and comment when they're doing the right thing. Develop positive rapport by remembering something about the student or something they said in the last lesson.

Try this ☞ | **Postive:negative**

Choose a student with SEBD. Draw two columns on a piece of paper. During your lesson, put a tick in one column for every negative interaction you have with that student, and a tick in the other for every positive interaction. The positive to negative ratio should be at least 5:1. If it isn't, how can you improve it?

Try this ☞ | **Catch me being good**

Set a behaviour target, for example: *I will focus on my own work*. Make a card with the title 'Catch me being good' (or 'Getting it right' for older students). Whenever you're walking around the class and you notice the student on-task, put a tick on the card.

✓ *Getting it right* | **Break the pattern**

Try to stay calm when faced with an angry, upset, or defiant student. Avoid being provoked and remain as positive as possible. Keep the focus on learning, ignore secondary behaviour (such as loud sighing), and redirect student behaviour rather than threatening sanctions.

Developing skills

Social and emotional

Students with SEBD need to develop their social and emotional skills. The English class offers many opportunities to do this. For example, students can be taught the words for basic emotions at an early level – 'sad', 'happy', 'tired', 'excited', etc. Older students can be taught a wider range, such as 'disappointed', 'surprised', and 'delighted'.

Try this ☞ | **What's my feeling?**

Ask one student to go out of the room and think of a feeling – or give them a word. The student comes back and mimes the feeling. The other students have to guess what it is.

Try this ☞   **Read my face**

Ask students to show you certain feelings by their facial expressions. For example, say: *Show me surprised/happy/bored*. Use this activity to check how your students are feeling at any stage in the lesson.

Try this ☞   **Feelings bingo**

Give out cards marked with five vertical columns and three horizontal rows – or get students to draw their own. Tell students to write feeling words in eight of the squares (younger students can draw faces with different expressions). Call out the words. If they have a word, students cover that square with a counter. They shout 'Bingo!' when they have covered a line or the full card.

Why this works ▐▐▐▶

> **Learning about emotions**
>
> Students with SEBD find it difficult to recognize emotions, and have a limited vocabulary for feelings in their L1. These activities give students a way to learn about their emotions and an opportunity to practise communicating them appropriately.

Stories as metaphors

Stories in English offer opportunities to explore how people react and think. Cartoons, everyday scenarios, and more developed stories all give students a chance to observe other people and ways of communicating. For students with SEBD, it can be easier to talk indirectly about characters in a story, play, or video than to talk about themselves – especially about their feelings and behaviour.

Try this ☞   **Inside and outside my head**

Use a story or a situation from your coursebook. Students look at the pictures and decide what the people are saying. Write this in a speech bubble. Now ask them what the people are thinking, explaining that it might not be the same. Write this in a thought bubble. Ask students what each person is feeling. Write this in a heart. Students share ideas, then write a story, dialogue, or role play using the characters they have created.

For younger students, do a role play at the front of the class. Show the pictures and hold up a big speech bubble, asking students to suggest ideas. Do the same with the thought and feeling bubbles.

Try this ☞   **Answer for me**

A student (A) stands at the front and represents a character from the coursebook. Two students (B and C) stand behind Student A to help her/him. The class then asks Student A questions, and Students B and C must answer the questions on behalf of Student A. If Student A agrees with their answers, s/he nods her/his head; if Student A thinks the answer is incorrect, s/he shakes her/his head and Students B and C must try again.

Why this works ▐▐▐▶ | **Developing empathy**

These activities teach students to empathize with each other by imagining character responses – for example, how they would feel in a certain situation and how they would show these feelings. Students learn to work together and understand each other better, and peer relationships are strengthened as a result.

Teacher self-care

Students with SEBD can affect a teacher's confidence and sense of competence. At times the teacher may feel rejected and disappointed when they can't manage the students in class. It can be difficult to build relationships with students who don't trust adults. It's vital for teachers to develop self-care and self-management strategies to be able to cope with students' difficult behaviour. If the adults can remain calm and supportive, the students will learn to respond differently.

1 Make sure you have a plan to manage your own stress levels and reactions to challenging students.
2 Work with a supportive colleague. Agree to meet regularly to discuss issues and to listen to each other.
3 Catch yourself in any negative or blaming self-talk and practise positive self-talk. Be kind to yourself and accept you are human.
4 Look for patterns of behaviour which are being enacted around students. It's possible to get caught up in students' emotions and responses. Find a way to break these patterns and to react differently.
5 Make sure you eat properly, exercise regularly, and get enough sleep.
6 Spend time doing things which energize you, and notice if you're spending too much time on activities which drain you.

11 Autism spectrum condition (ASC)

I wish the teacher wouldn't talk about me as if I'm not there. Just because I'm not looking at her doesn't mean I'm not listening.
PHILIPPE, AGED 8

Students like Philippe, who have autism spectrum condition (ASC), can find mainstream schools difficult because teachers may have little knowledge of ASC. The word 'autism' can make teachers assume there is a need for specialist care. In fact, the autism spectrum is wide, ranging from mild to severe. Some people with severe autism do need specialist care all their lives, but some with milder autism lead independent lives. You may have some of these students in your classes. You might also have students who have Asperger's syndrome, a form of autism.

Don't panic at the idea of teaching students with ASC. Be prepared to see the person behind the label. This chapter focuses on the teaching of students at the milder end of the autism spectrum and those with Asperger's syndrome. In this book the term autism spectrum condition (ASC) is used, but you may have heard the term autistic spectrum disorder (ASD).

Ask yourself

Does the terminology matter? What do you think when you hear the word 'autism'? What's the difference between a condition and a disorder?

What is ASC?

Students with ASC usually have difficulties to some extent in three areas. These are known as the **triad of impairments** and they affect:
• social interaction (relationships)
• language and communication (verbal and non-verbal)
• social imagination.

Asperger's syndrome is a form of autism affecting the way a person communicates or relates to others. People with Asperger's syndrome usually have fewer problems with language than those with autism. They can often speak fluently, although their language might sound formal and stilted. They don't usually have learning difficulties, but find social situations challenging.

Causes

The exact causes of autism are not known, but researchers believe there are a variety of factors, including a genetic component. It is not caused by poor diet or poor parenting. Parents/Carers often worry that they have done something wrong, so it's very important to be supportive and non-judgemental. Parents/Carers may have had to fight for services and support for their child and will welcome a positive and interested teacher.

Diagnosis

Diagnosis of autism should only be made by a qualified clinician. Teachers should be careful not to make assumptions based on the indicators below. These are only given as an explanation of the difficulties a student with ASC might have in class and to guide teachers who are wondering whether to refer a student for assessment.

Indicators

A student with ASC might have the following issues in class:

Social interaction
- difficulty understanding social rules – for example, standing too close to others or talking about something inappropriate
- difficulty understanding other people's feelings and expressing their own feelings
- often prefer to spend time on their own
- may appear clumsy due to difficulties with coordination
- may have sensory issues – for example, over-sensitive to light, noise, taste, smell, texture or under-sensitive to pain

Language and communication
- difficulty using or understanding facial expressions
- can often have a very literal understanding of language and problems
- difficulty understanding idioms, metaphors, and irony
- can sound too formal when speaking or appear ill-mannered
- may talk fluently, but won't always notice the reactions of other people – for example, when they lose interest in the conversation
- may talk obsessively about a special hobby or interest

Social imagination
- difficulty engaging in imaginative play and activities
- rigid thinking – for example, insisting that there is only one fair or right way to do things
- difficulty adapting to change – for example, timetable changes or a substitute teacher
- can be unaware of the potential dangers inherent in risky behaviour

Strengths

Students on the autism spectrum have strengths which you can build on in class. Get to know each student; find out as much as possible about their condition, their difficulties, and their strengths. The best people to help you with this are the parents/carers. They will want to work with you and share strategies. Find out if students use any pictures or signs for common words at home – for example, **Makaton** or **PECS**.

Students with ASC can have an excellent memory for facts and figures, and will often do well in exams which require this type of study, particularly in subjects of special interest to them. They are often logical and enjoy applying rules, so they can be good at ruled-based areas of study such as grammar. They are often strong visual learners who will benefit particularly from this style of learning.

Others may become very interested in a certain topic and be motivated to study high-level vocabulary items. Students at all levels of ability will thrive in a structured and well-organized work environment.

Try this ☞   **The expert**

Ask students to prepare a presentation in English on their special subject. Ask the rest of the class to prepare questions. Arrange for students to make their presentation, and allow enough time for questions and answers.

Try this ☞   **New words from old**

Ask students in pairs to make up as many words as possible from the letters in a long word, for example: 'Mediterranean' (net, rat, ran, red, tear, etc.). Award points for the number of letters in each correct word ('red' = three points, 'tear' = 4 points, etc.).

✓ *Getting it right*   **Special interests**

Ask parents/carers what their child's special interests are and discuss ways to use them in schoolwork. This will provide a highly motivating context for learning new language. For example, if a student is interested in trains, exploit this to teach numbers, colours, jobs, directions, etc. You can then gently broaden these fields of interest by introducing related topics or ideas.

Social interaction

Students with ASC often have difficulties forming relationships with their classmates. They may have difficulty understanding how their peers are feeling, and show no interest in what other people are saying. They can therefore appear rude and insensitive. They can also get very anxious in groups because they don't understand the unwritten social rules most of us take for granted. This means that they might not like typical English language class activities such as pair and group work, mingling activities, and discussions. To tackle this, allow students to occasionally work on their own, but alongside others who are doing a similar task. Students with ASC find it easier if the other person is next to them rather than facing them directly. Don't put pressure on them to make eye contact, but encourage it where possible.

Support and empathy

Try to create a cooperative and supportive classroom environment where difference is celebrated and students help each other. The English class offers opportunities to teach empathy, emotional understanding, and social skills in even the most mundane dialogues.

Use games as an opportunity to encourage turn-taking. Make sure the rules are clear, and try to avoid overly competitive games which can create anxiety. Ask other students to demonstrate how the game works and reinforce this by repeating instructions. For example, say: *Now it's your turn, Juan. Pick up a card like Maria and Blanca did.*

Be aware that students with ASC can be very sensitive to **sensory stimuli** such as loud noises, bright lights, or strong smells. It isn't always easy to identify what the triggers are for a particular student with ASC, but their reactions can be extreme.

Ask yourself

Do your students with ASC seem to change mood suddenly? What sensory triggers might be causing the change?

With permission from students and parent/carers, ask students to explain ASC to their peers (see page 15). Students with ASC have a different view of the world, but this is valuable and the other students can learn from it. When they understand the difficulties of students with ASC, they are usually supportive.

Try this ☞ **Name the feeling**

Make pairs of cards with 1) photos of people expressing different feelings (choosing words according to student age and ability) and 2) cards with the word which best describes the feelings. In groups, students sort the cards into matching pairs. Older students can play this game as 'Pelmanism' (see page 76).

Try this ☞ **Paying attention**

Keep a checklist of what interests students and what triggers positive or negative reactions.

Sensory triggers (positive):	Sensory triggers (negative):
• spinning or revolving objects	• bright lights and colours
• lining things up	• loud noises
• touching or smelling things	

FIGURE 11.1   *Checklist of student's interests*

Social skills

Help students with ASC to understand social skills by using commentary. Draw their attention to other students who are doing the right thing. For example, say: *Samar is waiting her turn quietly. Can you do that?* Notice when students with ASC are doing the right thing and praise them, describing appropriate behaviour explicitly. For example, say: *Well done for listening to your partner and speaking when they had finished. That's waiting your turn.*

Help students learn social conventions through role play of everyday situations such as 'shopping' or 'in the café' – typical contexts in many English language coursebooks. These situations are often presented through pictures and cartoons which are great for visual learners. They can also help with teaching idiomatic conversational English. Explain to students that role-playing is like practising for real life, so that when you find yourself in a real shop, you are well prepared for it.

Try this ☞ **Right/Wrong role plays**

Students prepare and perform two types of role play: 1) where people speak appropriately, and 2) where they're honest but not polite or respond in strange unpredictable ways. Exaggerate the difference. For example:

A: Hello, how are you?

B: What? Who are you?

A: I'm your new teacher.

B: Who cares. Go home.

Try this ☞ **Draw what you say**

Ask students to draw pictures to illustrate the literal and actual meanings of some English idioms. For example, for 'hurry up': 1) a picture of a student running up a ladder (literal and incorrect), and 2) a picture of a student rushing to finish their work (actual and correct).

Language and communication

Students with ASC have difficulties with language and communication in their L1, which can affect their learning of English. When listening, students may have problems understanding longer, complicated sentences. When speaking, they may miss communication signals such as bored facial expressions, and keep talking non-stop even after the other person has lost interest in the conversation. Sometimes their speech can sound stilted or odd, and the language they use may be over-formal.

Giving instructions

Reduce ambiguity and uncertainty when giving information and instructions by using precise classroom language wherever possible. For example, students may be confused by questions such as: *Who knows the answer?* They may be waiting for the person called 'Who' to answer or for their own name to be called. Say instead, *Simone, can you answer the question?*

✓ *Getting it right* **Fairness**

Be as consistent as possible. Be prepared to respond if a student with ASC questions your fairness. For example, they might ask why you told them to stop talking but didn't tell other students to stop. You can say: *I understand you're upset, but I want you to focus on yourself at the moment*.

Classroom environment

It's vital that you create as calm a classroom environment as possible. Ensure the student is sitting in a comfortable place and position. They might need to sit in the same place for every lesson. You could also create a quiet place for students to go to when they're becoming overly anxious. Make this a distraction-free zone.

Try this ☞   **A quiet space**

For younger children, use a small tent. Or use furniture such as bookcases to section off areas so that students can work away from noise or other children. Turn their desk around if necessary.

Suit activities to students' strengths

If possible, ask students before class which activities they like and which make them anxious. For example, multisensory activities can help students communicate more easily. When asking the class to work collaboratively, be aware that group and pair work aren't always the best ways to help students with ASC to learn. So consider sometimes allowing them access to a quiet space to complete activities.

Try this ☞   **Categorizing**

Categorizing activities are often popular with students with ASC. Older students can match words to meanings or sort out word or picture cards into categories. Younger children with more limited vocabulary can sort out objects according to their shape or colour.

Try this ☞   **Computers**

Working on a computer can provide a safe alternative to social groups for students with ASC. Word processors and simple graphics programs provide the opportunity to experiment, be creative, take risks, and 'undo' mistakes. Unlike people, computers always respond in the same way to requests and never object to repeating tasks. (See Chapter 6 for more ideas.)

Try this ☞   **Grammar buttons**

Teach students to use different coloured buttons (or blocks) for different parts of speech – for example, a red button for nouns, a blue button for verbs, etc. Give students sentences to colour-code with buttons and then practise saying them.

Social imagination

Social imagination involves being able to view the world from the perspective of others. It allows us to understand and predict other people's behaviour and what might happen next, make sense of abstract ideas, and to imagine situations outside our immediate daily routine.

Difficulties with social imagination mean that students with ASC have problems understanding other people's thoughts and actions, dealing with changes to routine and unfamiliar situations, and engaging with imaginative play or activities. It isn't true to say, however, that students with ASC lack imagination. They can be creative if the context is made clear and there is a logical element to the task.

Try this ☞ **Aliens**

Ask students to work in pairs. Give each student three pieces of paper and tell them to write a part of the body on each sheet. Collect the pieces of paper and then redistribute three to each student. Ask students to create an alien from the cut-up body part words. Tell them to draw it and to give it an identity – for example, decide on a name, age, home, etc.

Structure

Students with ASC need clear structure to help them manage their anxiety about daily routines. Be clear about expectations of behaviour. If possible, warn them about any changes to their routine or changes of activity in advance. Allow students to have their own mini poster of class rules and routines on their desk.

Try this ☞ **My classroom checklist**

Provide checklists of common classroom routines.

When I go into class, I:

 1 hang my coat up and then sit at my desk

 2 take out my pencil and write neatly in my book

 3 put my hand up when I want to ask a question.

FIGURE 11.2 *Student checklist for classroom routines*

Students with ASC respond well to visual input, so use a visual timetable to show the order of activities in the class (see Appendix 2, page 100). Knowing what is going to happen and when may help many students feel secure.

 **Getting it right**

Unstructured time

Many students with ASC find unstructured free time very difficult. If you have a 'choosing time' in your lesson, give students with ASC closed choices – for example, a list of activities they can work through or an ongoing project on a favourite topic.

12 Speech and language difficulties (SLD)

What are SLD?

A student with SLD might have problems in understanding what is said to them (receptive language), and/or the production of speech (**expressive language**). Difficulties vary from mild to severe. Students who can't make themselves understood or can't understand others often become frustrated in class and may start to misbehave. Poor or withdrawn behaviour can be an early indication that a student might have SLD.

Indicators

It can be difficult to identify speech and language difficulties in the English language classroom because many of the indicators occur naturally when a student is learning a new language. Students might have speech and language difficulties if they have noticeably more difficulty with:

- making themselves understood, due to problems with pronunciation and grammar (not caused by L1 interference)
- substituting one sound for another
- cluster phonemes, such as 'sl', 'sh', 'ch', 'sp'
- missing out the ends of words
- using tenses correctly
- understanding complex sentences, **non-literal** language, jokes, and sarcasm
- social use of language – for example, following instructions, turn-taking, understanding and responding in group discussions
- making and maintaining friendships and communicating feelings
- learning new words and remembering the right names for things, or using non-specific words in their L1, such as the equivalent of 'thingy' or 'stuff'
- understanding written language.

Ask yourself

Do you think that students with SLD are capable of learning an L2 such as English?

Causes

There are several potential causes of SLD. They are not usually connected to a student's intelligence, but often occur in conjunction with other specific learning difficulties such as dyslexia, dyspraxia, or ADHD. They are sometimes linked to conditions such as hearing loss, Down's syndrome, **cerebral palsy**, and autism.

Diagnosis

If you think that a student is having greater speech and language problems than you would expect at their age, listen to them talking in their L1, then discuss any concerns with the teachers of the student's L1 subjects. Use the list of indicators on page 87 as a discussion point. Then consider a referral to a speech therapist for an assessment of their difficulties. Speech and language therapists can usually suggest activities and support strategies for home and school.

Receptive language difficulties

Some students have problems with the way they hear and process language, affecting their ability to understand what others are saying and to respond appropriately. Students can have **pragmatic language difficulties** where they understand the actual words being said, but don't understand the meaning and social function of the language. They have trouble understanding non-literal language such as humour and metaphor (see Chapter 8 on dyspraxia and Chapter 11 on ASC for more information on pragmatic language difficulties).

Support student understanding in the following ways:
- Speak naturally and clearly. Don't talk more loudly or more slowly as if the student is less intelligent.
- Seat students near you so they can see your face for expressions and lip-reading and, if possible, so the light falls on your face and lips.
- Remember not to speak with your back to students when you're writing on the board.
- Keep background noise down as much as possible.

Try this  **Who's speaking?**

Attract the student's attention by saying their name, or if appropriate, tapping on their shoulder and saying their name before speaking to them. During class discussion, indicate where a student is speaking from. For example, say: *Carlos at the back, what do you think?*

Students will need more thinking time to understand information in class. Be patient when waiting for their answers to give them time to process your language. Remind other students of the rule: *We all wait quietly when someone needs thinking time.* If a student doesn't understand, repeat what you said and use the same language. Don't paraphrase because it will confuse the student more.

✓ Getting it right   **Visual support**

Support student understanding by using visual cue cards and real objects to illustrate important language and information – for example, visual timetables (see Appendix 2, page 100), posters with keywords and phrases, or a word bank on the wall. Let the student use a visual signal to show if they haven't understood something – for example, a thumbs up or down.

Students with SLD often have greater than normal difficulty in discriminating between certain sounds in English. Give them multisensory practice in recognizing the difference between confusing sounds by using games which all students are likely to enjoy.

Try this ☞ **Jump the line**

Students stand in a line in the middle of the classroom. Choose some words which students find difficult to discriminate between, for example, words beginning with /b/ and /v/. Tell students to jump to the right if they hear a word beginning with /b/ and to the left if they hear one beginning with /v/.

Try this ☞ **Run and touch**

Put up some picture cards of target words on the board. Divide students into teams and ask them to line up facing the board. Call out a word. A member of each team must run and touch the card which corresponds to the word or sound you called out.

Remember that receptive language difficulties might be a sign of a hearing impairment. Students can be embarrassed and reluctant to tell the teacher that they can't hear very well and it can be difficult for the teacher to recognise their needs. They sometimes only show this with misbehaviour – for example, talking loudly and ignoring instructions.

Ask yourself

Have you got any students who always sit at the back, talk loudly, and don't seem to listen? Could they have a hearing problem?

Expressive language difficulties

Some students have problems with the muscular movements needed to form words. They have trouble producing certain sounds and simply leave them out, or substitute one sound for another. This can make students difficult to understand.

 **Getting it right**

Students as teachers

If students have had speech therapy in their L1, they may already be aware of the physical actions involved in producing sounds. They can help their classmates to learn pronunciation by imitating the movements of the lips and tongue.

Students can also have difficulty putting words in the right order in a sentence or telling stories with the events in the right sequence. Students may use inappropriate grammatical structures, and their speech may sound immature for their age. They may find it difficult to recall and use vocabulary.

Many activities in the English language classroom help students develop their general expressive language skills. For example:
- putting a sequence of pictures in order and retelling the story or events
- putting words in a sentence in the correct order

- putting a dialogue in order
- matching words to pictures
- learning functional phrases in English – for example: *I'm sorry, I don't understand. Can you repeat that, please?*
- fluency activities which focus on communicating meaning rather than using the correct words.

Try this ☞   **Our group sentence**

Put students in groups and give each student in the group one word on a piece of paper from a cut-up sentence. Ask them to remember their word and then give their piece of paper back to you. Tell students to arrange themselves in the correct order according to their sentence by saying their words to each other. Try not to intervene so that students have to listen and talk to each other.

Establish some class routines for listening and paying attention. Explain to the class that it's important to be attentive and look at someone when they're talking to you, and not to interrupt.

Try this ☞   **Talking pen**

Make a rule that students can only talk in discussions if they're holding a special pen as a 'microphone'. Only the holder of the pen can speak, and the others shouldn't interrupt.

Give students opportunities to respond in different ways in class. For example, if they have difficulty explaining things in the right order, allow them to think first of bullet points of what they want to say, which they can then put in sequence on a timeline. Or use the 'Think, pair, share' activity (see page 28). When you want students to make a choice or express an opinion, offer closed choices – for example: *Do you want the red or blue pen?* rather than *Which pen do you want?* Allow students to respond in non-verbal ways such as with mini whiteboards and drawings. (See Chapter 4 for more on responses.)

Communicating needs

Communicating their needs to teachers and classmates can be very frustrating for students with SLD. You can help reduce this frustration by allowing them to work in smaller groups or pairs. Discuss in class the ways students can help each other, and seat students with SLD with able and sympathetic classmates. If you can't understand students, it isn't helpful to pretend you can. Say: *I'm sorry, I don't understand. Please can you say it again?* Also, be aware if you weren't listening properly. Ask other students to help you, because sometimes they have a better understanding of each other.

Try this ☞ **Classroom poster**

Use a classroom poster with suggested solutions to a communication problem.

> *In our class, if a student is stuck for a word, we can ...*
>
> **say ...** *Have you forgotten the word? Would you like some help?*
>
> **repeat ...** what they said and give a lead in. *So high in the sky you saw a plane ...*
>
> **ask ...** the student to describe the word they're thinking of.
>
> **ask ...** *Is it a long or short word?*
>
> **give ...** or ask for the first sound.

FIGURE 12.1   *Classroom poster with solutions to communication problems*

Try this ☞ **Conversation by numbers**

Students have a 'conversation' in pairs using only numbers and intonation to convey meaning. Demonstrate at the front with a pair of volunteers. For example:

Student A: One. *(in the tone of a greeting)*
Student B: One ... two, three, four? *(as if asking 'How are you?')*
Student A: Five, Six. *(in a flat, slow way as if to say 'Oh, OK.')*

This shows students that meaning can be conveyed even when you don't know the right words or forget them.

Try this ☞ **Right word, wrong accent**

If students are having problems with remembering and pronouncing a word, ask them to say it with their L1 accent and to exaggerate its 'wrongness' as much as they can. Then ask them to try again with English pronunciation. They usually perform better!

Developing vocabulary

As with all students with SEN, students with SLD will benefit from targeted strategies to learn vocabulary. They can learn these techniques in the English class and transfer ideas to help their speech and language in their L1.

Ideas include:
- a personal vocabulary box of key words on picture cards
- a key vocabulary word bank on the wall or on the desk with visual reminders of meaning
- games which reinforce memory (matching pairs, etc.)

Try this ☞ **Clapping syllables**

Ask students to count out the number of syllables in a word, then clap each syllable, clapping loudest on the stressed syllable.

Try this ☞ **Consonant clusters**

Show **consonant clusters** in colour, for example: **ch**urch, **ch**ips. Ask students to cut up words keeping the clusters together. Create gestures and sounds to help students remember the cluster, for example: *cl...* (click fingers), *pl...* (make a plopping noise), *ch...* (make a 'train chugging along a track' gesture).

Try this ☞ **Backchaining**

Choose a word students are having problems pronouncing. Divide the word into sections and say it in reverse. So for 'shopping', say: *ing ... ping ... opping ... hopping ... shopping*.

Why this works ⫸

> **Brain distractions**
>
> Reinforcing through gesture and saying things in unusual ways distracts the brain from difficulties and sometimes stops students from feeling so anxious about producing the sounds.
> Students need support in recalling and using vocabulary at the right time. But they also need to develop fluency strategies which allow them to communicate meaning without knowing the exact vocabulary. This shows students with SLD that they don't necessarily need to know the precise words to be able to communicate.

Try this ☞ **Alphabet trigger**

When students are stuck for a word, teach them to scroll through the alphabet in their heads or look at the alphabet on the wall to find the first letter of the word. This often triggers recall of the word.

Try this ☞ **Taboo**

Give groups of students a situation they need to practise, such as asking for directions to the park. They can't use the word 'park', but they can say anything else and use gestures and drawings. Other students have to guess what they're asking.

13 Gifted and talented students

> I'm good at English and love learning new words, but sometimes lessons are really long and boring. I get impatient and shout out answers, which annoys the teacher. I hate making mistakes, but don't like checking my work.
>
> ALAIN, AGED 10

Who are gifted and talented students?

Alain is a gifted and talented student, which means he has abilities above the standard expected of a student his age. In this chapter we will look at the types of students in this category and teaching strategies which might help them.

There is, however, no general agreement about what the term 'gifted' and 'talented' means. Its definition varies according to country, culture, and even school. In this book we define 'gifted and talented' as follows:

> Gifted and talented is the term applied to those young people who are achieving, or who have the potential to achieve, at a level significantly beyond the rest of their peer group. 'Gifted' describes students who have the ability to excel academically in one or more subjects such as English, drama, or technology. 'Talented' describes students who have the ability to excel in practical skills such as sport, leadership, or artistic performance. These students may well follow a vocational training pathway to accreditation and employment.

Ask yourself

Do you agree with this definition? Does your country have a different one? Do gifted and talented students really need extra support?

Indicators

It isn't always easy to identify gifted and talented students, because their abilities and skills vary immensely often across subjects. A gifted and talented student might not always stand out from the rest of the class. Some students are confident and keen to show their abilities, but others hide their abilities in order to fit in.

Signs that students are gifted in your subject are that they:
- focus and concentrate for long periods of time, but may become impatient and irritable when concentration is interrupted
- learned to read early and have an extensive vocabulary
- get good marks in tests and personal projects but don't do so well in classwork

- rush work and finish quickly in order to get onto something else or may be perfectionists and don't like making mistakes
- are curious and ask a lot of questions, or may be bored and/or disruptive in class
- absorb and recall information easily and can quickly grasp concepts, make links, and generalize
- are intellectually and emotionally mature and show interest in the adult world – for example, current affairs
- are keen to improve institutions and systems; for example, they may be critical of school and/or sensitive to injustice.

Strengths

Gifted and talented students have a range of strengths, as identified above. They will apply themselves to an exceptionally high standard in subjects in which they excel, and can show good leadership qualities if encouraged to do so.

 *Getting it right*

Talent spotting

See beyond the behaviour of students who say lessons are boring or who rush through work carelessly. Misbehaviour can be a sign of lack of challenge and interest. Look for strengths and try to use them in class.

Types of behaviour in class

Although some gifted and talented students are comfortable with their different learning abilities and are confident, independent learners, others can struggle to fit in. They may hide their abilities in order to be accepted by their peers, challenge authority, and underachieve in class – or become angry and depressed if they are not stretched and their talents are not recognized. Some gifted and talented students have another special educational need or disability in addition to being gifted and talented. They can become demotivated if the school focuses on their weaknesses and not their strengths.

Ask yourself

Do you recognize any of your students in these descriptions? Are they achieving their potential? What can you do to meet their needs?

Try this 👉 **The examiner's mind**

Ask students to write a test on a topic you've recently covered in class. Give them the marking criteria and ask them to write the test with this in mind.

Try this 👉 **Class resources**

Ask students to develop resources for the whole class – for example, making a class dictionary, creating wall displays, writing book reviews for the class library, or even setting up a class newsletter or blog which they can edit.

Try this ☞ **Class contract**

Give students responsibility for drawing up and maintaining rules for the class contract. Encourage them to consider rights and responsibilities and to run a regular class meeting about issues.

Try this ☞ **Mood monitor**

Ask a student to act as the mood monitor of the group. They should keep a check on how everyone in the class is feeling. This can be done with a barometer which shows a scale of mood, from not good to very good. If they notice the mood is not good, the student should move the pointer on the barometer to show the teacher.

The five intensities

There are five areas in which gifted and talented students might excel; these are called the five intensities.

Emotional

Students have strong feelings and complex emotions. They can express feelings easily and empathize with the feelings of others.

Try this ☞ **Words I like/don't like**

When reviewing vocabulary, ask the students to divide the words into words they like the sound of and words they don't like the sound of. Higher-level students can discuss in English why they like or don't like the word, but lower-level students can discuss in their L1.

Intellectual

Students can concentrate for long periods of time, have active, curious minds, and enjoy problem-solving, logical word games, and puzzles.

Try this ☞ **Codes and spies**

Ask students in groups to design a code for spies to use when sending messages in English. This could be a visual code where one symbol equals a letter. For example: § = A, £ = B, etc. They should design their code and write a message to another group who try to decode it.

Sensual

Students are very aware of their senses and are easily affected by textures, smells, and tastes. They love music, art, and language.

Try this ☞ **Draw my music**

Choose five very different pieces of music. Play each one and ask students to draw what it makes them think about. When they have five drawings, ask them to work alone or in groups to make up a story which includes all the pictures.

Imaginational

Students have vivid imaginations, and they love metaphor and fantasy. They enjoy reading and writing stories and doing imaginative tasks.

Try this ☞ **Similes and metaphors**

Ask students to review vocabulary by making unusual metaphorical connections. They should compare items from different vocabulary lists. For example: *A school ... is like ... a tiger ... because ... it can be exciting.*

Psychomotor

Students are extremely active, energetic, and well coordinated. They're passionate and enthusiastic and often talk very fast. They enjoy kinaesthetic games and speaking activities.

Try this ☞ **Volume control drilling**

Ask students to repeat target language in different ways (shout, whisper, sing, say in funny voices, laugh, etc.). Conduct the drill by pretending you have a remote control for volume (you could use a real one). Give students a chance to be in charge of this and to think of new ways to do it.

Differentiation

Questions

One of the easiest ways to differentiate is with questions. Bloom's taxonomy is a classification system useful for formulating questions to suit different levels of student ability. It classifies levels of understanding into lower order thinking skills (**LOTS**) and higher order thinking skills (**HOTS**).

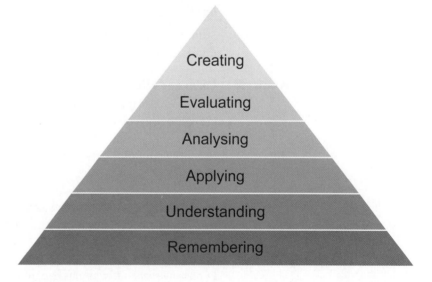

FIGURE 13.1   *Bloom's taxonomy*

LOTS are very useful for checking that students remember and understand information, and include questions beginning with *Who, When, Where, What,* and *Why.* You probably use them in the classroom for this purpose.

HOTS provide opportunities for critical thinking and creative problem-solving, and are ideal for stretching and challenging gifted and talented students. Bloom identified four levels of understanding:

1 Applying knowledge to a different context – for example, using known language in a new context.

Try this ☞ **My first English book**

Ask the students to write short stories or cartoons for younger, lower-level readers. This allows them to help others and to show their writing skills in a new context. They can work on this in a group, and some of the group can draw the illustrations.

2 Analysing information by breaking it down in parts to find patterns and relationships – for example, analysing the difference in meaning if sentences are reordered. Sample questions: *What's the difference between … ? How could you combine these … ?*

Try this ☞ **Expanding sentences**

Write a short sentence on the board. For example: *I am a girl.* Ask students to give you one or two words to make a new sentence. For example: *I am a young girl.* Keep asking them to give you one or two words until they run out of ways to add to the sentence.

I am a young Italian girl. → *I am a happy young Italian girl.*

Variation: Older students can do this as a round; one student starts and the next student adds one or two words.

3 Evaluating information to develop opinions and form judgements – for example, evaluating a character's personality or actions in a story. Sample questions: *Do you agree … ? Which is best in your opinion … ?*

Try this ☞ **Hot seating**

Ask students to choose a character from a story or your coursebook who they think is the most interesting or most valuable to the plot. Tell the student to sit in front of the class in the 'hot seat' as that character and to convince the other students of their importance.

4 Creating something new and learning to think in a more abstract way – for example, inventing something or making unusual connections between words.

Sample questions: *How would you design … ? What could you change to improve … ?*

Try this ☞ **Task design**

Ask students to create a practice activity which encourages students to make unusual connections. For example, when teaching vocabulary, ask them to create a memory strategy to share with the rest of the class which connects the words to an unusual visual trigger.

Change the outcome

When planning class activities, add an extra twist which changes the outcome – for example, by writing texts for a specific audience, or from the perspective of a particular character in a book. If the class is learning about animals, students could present a news report on a zoo.

Try this ☞ **The editor**

In a writing activity, ask some students to be editors. Tell them they have been asked to cut the writing down to a certain word limit. If possible, teach them how to edit using the tracking and editing tools on the computer.

Try this ☞ **Character tea party**

Choose a chapter in your coursebook which has introduced different characters, perhaps through stories or dialogues. Tell students to pick their favourite characters and to pretend to be attending a tea party as that character, meeting others and talking in character. Younger children can be encouraged to dress up.

Self-access materials

Students need to learn to deal with their impatience when the lesson is not going as quickly as they wish, or when they are not getting enough of your attention. Self-access activities (see page 37) are very useful in teaching your gifted and talented students, particularly open-ended longer-term projects of interest. Manage self-access by providing a weekly or monthly agenda of tasks for the student so that they know what they can get on with if they have finished other work.

Try this ☞ **Reading activities**

- Write a letter to the author of a book you've enjoyed.
- Create a bestseller list for your ten favourite books!
- Rewrite the ending of a book you've read and make it end in a different way.
- Create an original dialogue between two characters from a book you've read.

You also need to remain patient and positive in the face of any interruptions or bored looks. Try to encourage students to think of ways to manage their own frustration.

Try this ☞ **Self-management aide-memoire**

Get students to write down the tips they need to remember to manage their own impatience. Put this on a card and laminate it.

- When the teacher doesn't give me 'special work', think of another way to use what I've learned – or think of how to teach it to someone.

- Instead of shouting out, have some spare paper to write my answers on.

- If I have a speaking partner, talk to them first before telling the class.

- Remember to check work. Put a special mark at the bottom to tell the teacher that I've checked it.

FIGURE 13.2   *Student self-management aide-memoire*

Appendices

Appendix 1: Definitions of types of SEN

Additional educational needs (AEN) The needs of students who require extra provision for their learning in school.

Asperger's syndrome A condition on the higher functioning end of the autism spectrum which affects the way learners communicate or relate to others. They usually have fewer problems with language than those with autism, but have difficulties with social situations.

Attention deficit hyperactivity disorder (ADHD) Learners find it difficult to sit still, concentrate, and speak at appropriate times.

Autism spectrum condition (ASC) Also known as autism spectrum disorder (ASD). Learners have a pervasive developmental disorder, ranging on a spectrum from mild to severe, usually causing problems with social communication, motor skills, and sometimes intellectual functioning.

Dyslexia Learners have difficulties with the skills involved in reading and spelling, phonological awareness, verbal memory, and processing speed.

Dyspraxia A developmental coordination difficulty. Learners have difficulty coordinating the body and muscles to perform the actions needed to carry out tasks. They can have problems with social skills, concentration, perception, and organization.

Gifted and talented Learners who have a particular talent or ability in one or more subjects and whose ability is significantly greater than their peers of the same age.

Social, emotional, and behavioural difficulties (SEBD) Learners have problems behaving appropriately in class.

Special educational needs (SEN) Students with SEN need special educational provision for their learning difficulty.

Appendix 2: Visual timetable

Friday

Morning activities

Register

Exercise

Maths

Break time

Planning time

Writing

Lunchtime

Afternoon activities

English

ICT

Snack time

Reading

History

Art

Home time

Appendix 3: Mind map

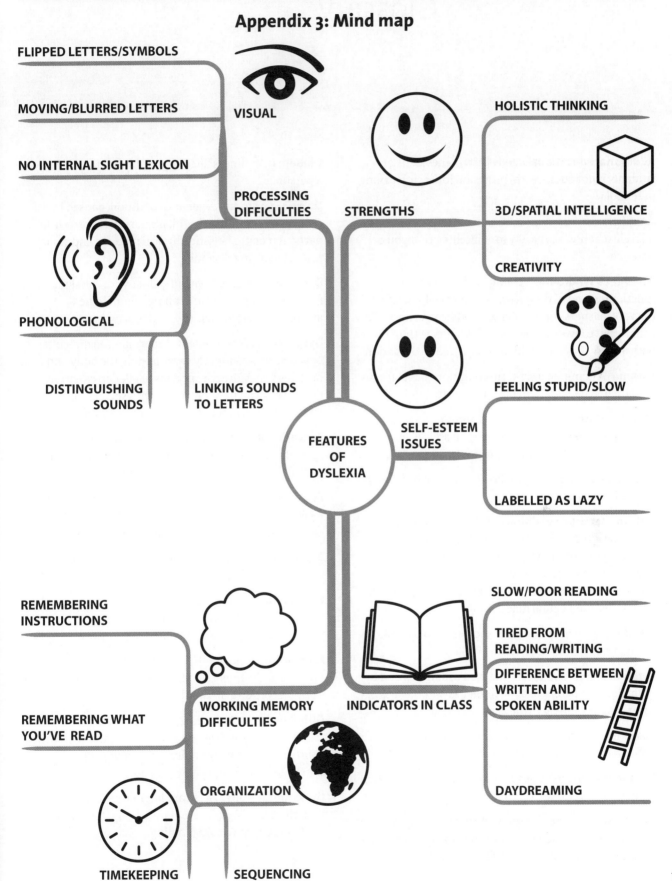

FLIPPED LETTERS/SYMBOLS

MOVING/BLURRED LETTERS

VISUAL

NO INTERNAL SIGHT LEXICON

PROCESSING DIFFICULTIES

STRENGTHS

HOLISTIC THINKING

3D/SPATIAL INTELLIGENCE

CREATIVITY

PHONOLOGICAL

DISTINGUISHING SOUNDS

LINKING SOUNDS TO LETTERS

FEATURES OF DYSLEXIA

SELF-ESTEEM ISSUES

FEELING STUPID/SLOW

LABELLED AS LAZY

REMEMBERING INSTRUCTIONS

REMEMBERING WHAT YOU'VE READ

WORKING MEMORY DIFFICULTIES

INDICATORS IN CLASS

SLOW/POOR READING

TIRED FROM READING/WRITING

DIFFERENCE BETWEEN WRITTEN AND SPOKEN ABILITY

ORGANIZATION

DAYDREAMING

TIMEKEEPING

SEQUENCING

Glossary

Additional educational needs (AEN) The needs of students who require extra provision for their learning in school.

Anaphylaxis A serious, sometimes life-threatening allergic reaction – typically to something that you eat or touch.

Asperger's syndrome A condition on the higher functioning end of the autism spectrum which affects the way learners communicate or relate to others. They usually have fewer problems with language than those with autism, but have difficulties with social situations.

Asthma A common long-term condition that can cause coughing, wheezing, and breathlessness.

Attention deficit hyperactivity disorder (ADHD) Learners find it difficult to sit still, concentrate, and speak at appropriate times.

Auditory learners People who like to learn by listening and talking.

Autism spectrum condition (ASC) Also known as autism spectrum disorder (ASD). Learners have a pervasive developmental disorder, ranging on a spectrum from mild to severe, usually causing problems with social communication, motor skills, and sometimes intellectual functioning.

Blending Hearing phonemes and being able to merge them together to make words.

Cerebral palsy A medical condition usually caused by brain damage before or at birth that causes the loss of control of movement in the arms and legs.

Chunking A strategy that helps students break down difficult text into more manageable parts.

Consonant clusters Consonants which occur together with no vowel between them, for example, 'sp', 'ch', 'pl'.

Developmental coordination difficulty Problems with coordinating the movements needed in everyday life – for example, eating with a knife and fork.

Diabetes An illness affecting the blood sugar levels of a person.

Down's syndrome A genetic condition, caused by a chromosome fault, in which a person is born with particular characteristic physical features and some level of learning disability.

Dyslexia Learners have difficulties with the skills involved in reading and spelling, phonological awareness, verbal memory, and processing speed.

Dyspraxia A developmental coordination difficulty. Learners have difficulty coordinating the body and muscles to perform the actions needed to carry out tasks. They can have problems with social skills, concentration, perception, and organization.

Educational psychologist A psychologist who is specially trained to assess pupils' special educational needs.

Epilepsy A disorder of the nervous system that causes a person to become unconscious suddenly, often with convulsions (or involuntary muscular contractions).

Expressive language The language we produce through speaking or writing.

Fight or flight A survival response which happens when we are under extreme threat or facing danger; the brain responds by prompting us to fight or run away.

Fine motor skills Small movements that use the muscles of the fingers, toes, wrists, lips, and tongue; for example, picking up small objects.

Gifted and talented Learners who have a particular talent or ability in one or more subjects and where their ability is significantly greater than their peers of the same age.

Gross motor skills These are larger movements made with the arms, legs, feet, or entire body; for example, crawling, running, and jumping.

Holistic thinkers People who understand a system by sensing its large-scale patterns and reacting to them.

Homonym A word that is spelt like another word (or pronounced like it) but which has a different meaning.

Homophone A word that is pronounced like another word but has a different spelling or meaning.

HOTS Higher Order Thinking Skills of remembering and understanding.

Internal sight lexicon Words which we hold in our memory and recognize by sight without needing to sound them out.

Kinaesthetic Learning through physical activity and through feelings – for example, by moving around, touching and doing things, or having chances to express your feelings about activities.

Left-brain The left side of the brain is associated with linear and analytical thought.

LOTS Lower Order Thinking Skills of remembering and understanding.

Makaton A method of communication using pictures and symbols.

Marking criteria A list of descriptors of standards which helps a teacher to mark work.

Mindful breathing Giving attention to the movement of the abdomen when breathing in and out.

NGO (Non-governmental organization) An organization that is not part of a government or a for-profit business.

Non-literal Not using or taking words in their usual or most basic sense.

Occupational therapists Professionals who help patients recover after illness or injury by giving them special activities to do.

Overlearn Continue to practise new information in different ways and contexts until it becomes automatic.

PECS The Picture Exchange Communication System, a form of augmentative and alternative communication.

Peers People similar in age, background, or social status.

Pragmatic language difficulties Problems with social use of language; misunderstanding how we use language in social interactions and communication.

Productive language Written and spoken language.

Receptive language The language we understand through listening or reading.

Reptilian brain The oldest part of the brain responsible for survival responses.

Screen masking Highlighting areas of text on the computer screen in different colours in order to make it easier to read.

Scribe A person who does the writing in an examination for someone who has special educational needs, for example because they have dyslexia or dyspraxia.

Segmenting Breaking apart the different sounds that make up a word.

Sensory stimuli The stimulation of any of the five senses.

Social, emotional, and behavioural difficulties (SEBD) Learners have problems behaving appropriately in class.

Special educational needs (SEN) Students with SEN require special educational provision for their learning difficulty.

Speech and language therapists People who help those who have problems in speaking clearly, for example, in pronouncing particular sounds.

Triad of impairments The three areas of difficulty for people with ASC: social interaction, language and communication, social imagination.

Visual learners People who like to learn by seeing and imagining things. They often think in pictures.

Visual timetable A timetable which has symbols and pictures to represent different lessons and activities.

Useful websites

ADHD
Russell A. Barkley:
www.russellbarkley.org

ASC
The National Autistic Society:
www.autism.org.uk

Assistive technology
AbilityNet:
www.abilitynet.org.uk

Clicker communicator:
www.cricksoft.com

Dance Mat Typing:
www.bbc.co.uk/guides/z3c6tfr

Dyslexia Help:
http://dyslexiahelp.umich.edu

EduApps:
www.eduapps.org

Education Place:
www.eduplace.com

Kar2ouche:
http://creativeedutech.com/products/kar2ouche/

Memrise:
www.memrise.com

Quizlet:
https://quizlet.com

SEMERC:
www.semerc.com

SEN teacher resources:
www.senteacher.org

Spritz Inc:
www.spritzinc.com

Teach Your Monster to Read:
www.teachyourmonstertoread.com

Twinkl SEN:
www.twinkl.co.uk/resources/
specialeducationalneeds-sen

Visual Stress Test:
www.visualstresstest.com

Wordshark:
www.wordshark.co.uk

Dyslexia
British Dyslexia Association:
www.bdadyslexia.org.uk

Dypraxia
Dyspraxia Foundation:
www.dyspraxiafoundation.org.uk

General SEN
Centre for Studies on Inclusive Education (CSIE):
www.csie.org.uk

National Association for Special Educational Needs (NASEN):
www.nasen.org.uk

SEN teacher resources:
www.senteacher.org

Teaching English:
www.teachingenglish.org.uk

Times Educational Supplement:
www.tes.co.uk

SEBD
SEBDA:
www.sebda.org/sebd

Speech and language
Afasic:
www.afasic.org.uk

The British Stammering Association:
www.stammering.org

Websites to buy resources
Stass publications:
www.stass.co.uk

Taskmaster:
www.taskmasteronline.co.uk